Hiring the Best Staff for Your School

Hiring the Best Staff for Your School moves beyond typical hiring tools—résumés, applications, transcripts, portfolios, and artifacts—and adds effective strategies to the educational leader's recruiting and hiring toolbox. Jetter hones in on the most crucial but often neglected element of talent searches—knowing candidates' attitudes and dispositions about students, learning and instruction, leadership, and other crucial educational topics which affect schools today—and provides an innovative model for hiring the best candidates. This book presents a recruitment and hiring process that uses narratives to help school and district leaders delve deeper into understanding the emotions, ideas, reactions, and problem-solving insights of candidates. The ready-to-use resources found in this book, including real examples of the narrative process in action, dialogues, and as a training process, are easy to implement and will strengthen the hiring process to ensure that you recruit and retain the best staff members for any position within your school or district.

Rick Jetter is an Educational Consultant, motivational speaker, and Director of Business Development at a leading educational resources company in New York State. He has been an educator for 17 years, as a teacher, assistant principal, principal, assistant superintendent, and superintendent of schools.

**Other Eye On Education Books Available from Routledge
(www.routledge.com/eyeoneducation)**

7 Ways to Transform the Lives of Wounded Students
Joe Hendershott

Five Critical Leadership Practices: The Secret to High-Performing Schools
Ruth C. Ash and Pat H. Hodge

Mentoring is a Verb: Strategies for Improving College and Career Readiness
Russ Olwell

How to Make Data Work: A Guide for Educational Leaders
Jenny Grant Rankin

A School Leader's Guide to Implementing the Common Core: Inclusive Practices for All Students
Gloria Campbell-Whatley, Dawson Hancock, and David M. Dunaway

What Connected Educators Do Differently
Todd Whitaker, Jeffrey Zoul, and Jimmy Casas

BRAVO Principal! Building Relationships with Actions that Value Others, 2nd Edition
Sandra Harris

Get Organized! Time Management for School Leaders, 2nd Edition
Frank Buck

The Educator's Guide to Writing a Book: Practical Advice for Teachers and Leaders
Cathie E. West

Data, Data Everywhere: Bringing All The Data Together for Continuous School Improvement, 2nd Edition
Victoria Bernhardt

Hiring the Best Staff for Your School

How to Use Narrative to Improve Your Recruiting Process

Rick Jetter

Routledge
Taylor & Francis Group
NEW YORK AND LONDON

First published 2016
by Routledge
711 Third Avenue, New York, NY 10017

and by Routledge
2 Park Square, Milton Park, Abingdon, Oxon, OX14 4RN

Routledge is an imprint of the Taylor & Francis Group, an informa business

© 2016 Taylor & Francis

The right of Rick Jetter to be identified as author of this work has been asserted by him in accordance with sections 77 and 78 of the Copyright, Designs and Patents Act 1988.

All rights reserved. No part of this book may be reprinted or reproduced or utilised in any form or by any electronic, mechanical, or other means, now known or hereafter invented, including photocopying and recording, or in any information storage or retrieval system, without permission in writing from the publishers.

Trademark notice: Product or corporate names may be trademarks or registered trademarks, and are used only for identification and explanation without intent to infringe.

Library of Congress Cataloging in Publication Data
Names: Jetter, Rick, author.
Title: Hiring the best staff for your school : how to use narrative to improve your recruiting process / Rick Jetter.
Description: New York, NY : Routledge, [2016] | Includes bibliographical references.
Identifiers: LCCN 2015034362| ISBN 9781138125469 (hardback) | ISBN 9781138125476 (pbk.) | ISBN 9781315647494 (ebook)
Subjects: LCSH: Teachers—Selection and appointment—United States. | Teachers—Recruiting—United States.
Classification: LCC LB2835.25 .J48 2016 | DDC 379.1/57—dc23
LC record available at http://lccn.loc.gov/2015034362

ISBN: 978-1-138-12546-9 (hbk)
ISBN: 978-1-138-12547-6 (pbk)
ISBN: 978-1-315-64749-4 (ebk)

Typeset in Optima
by Swales & Willis Ltd, Exeter, Devon, UK

Contents

Preface   viii
What Is Different About This Book?   ix
How This Book Will be Useful to You   x
Acknowledgments   xiii
Meet the Author   xv

1 Putting the "Best" Back Into Hiring   1
Adding an Additional Multiple Measure for Hiring the "Best"   2
Human Feelings Elicit Attitudes   3
Proven Success   4
What Does the Word "Best" Really Mean?   5
References   6

2 Some Challenges With Traditional Educational Talent Searches   7
Traditional Application Documents   9
   The Résumé   9
   The Application   12
   College Transcripts   14
   Certifications   17
   Letters of Reference (a.k.a. The Placement Folder)   19
   The Cover Letter   20
   The Portfolio   21
   The Interview   22
   What Does That Question Really Search For?   23

Contents

3 Why Narratives?   27
Narratives "Counting" as Research   27
Narrative Theory and Practical Uses   30
Narratives That Build Meaning From Exchanges With the "Other"   31
Narratives Build Socialized Intertextuality and Identity Shifting   32
Narratives and the Identity Behind Our Displayed Attitudes   34
Narratives Describe Position, Agency, and Truth   36
Who Cares About Educators' Stories?   40
Hiring Practices and Narrative Theory   42
References   43

4 Getting Your Resources and Team Ready   46
Selecting the Narrative Style and Tool   47
Selecting the Narrative Writer   48
Using the Four SLAC Creeds   51
   Students   52
   Learning   54
   Achievement   55
   Culture   56
Deeper Interviewing   57
Interview Questions That Mine for Attitudes   59
Putting It All Together   61

5 Thinking About Your Recruitment Process and Who Is Exempt   63
Criteria First; Screening Second   63
Screening Second; Post-Recruitment Third   64
No One Is Exempt From Narrating Their Own Worlds   66
What About Library Media Specialists?   67
What About School Leaders?   68
Working Through Embellishment   71

6 Assessing Candidates for Attitudes and Dispositions   73
Designing Rubrics   76

Deciding on an Ideal Response to a Story: Establishing
a Benchmark Narrative   79
A Comparative Analysis of Narratives: One Example   83
Weighing in: Aligning the Multiple Measures of Hiring
the "Best"   88
Narrative as a Learning Tool for All: Reflection and
Professional Development   92
Reference   95

7 Hiring the Best in the Elm Grove Central School District   96
The Demographics and History of Elm Grove   96
The "Old" Hiring Process   98
New Hiring Opportunities and Narrative Interests   101
Hiring the Best Business Teacher   103
Hiring the Best Assistant Principal   109
The Results   114

8 Hiring the Best in the Gardenville City School District   119
The Demographics and History of Gardenville   119
The Story of Canton Elementary School   120
Hiring the Best Reading Teacher   121
Hiring the Best Social Worker   125
Narrative Power   127

9 PPCs and FAQs   130
Pluses   130
Potentials   133
Concerns and FAQs   134
Words of Advice   136

10 Finding the "Best" by the End of Your Hiring Process   138
Creating a Viral Process: Looking Outside the
School Walls   138

Preface

We all have attitudes about our craft, but we sometimes forget to ask others about those attitudes when we search to hire the best staff members for our schools. I sat on my first interview committee when I was a first-year English teacher. It was interesting, to say the least. The committee interviewed eight candidates for one teacher-aide position. I wasn't really sure how my school district narrowed down our applicant pool to eight candidates.

Certainly, the principal was effective, the teachers sitting next to me were effective, but I felt like I knew very little about the candidates we interviewed.

What I mean is that I knew nothing about their attitudes about covering the lunch breaks of other teacher aides, their dispositions and beliefs about working with challenging students who might have an outburst for an unknown reason. All I knew was the candidates' answers to 10, basic interview questions, one of which was, "What are you doing professionally to stay sharp?"

I was confused. If all the candidates on that day were in a good mood or a bad mood, I wouldn't really know. They all smiled and gave satisfactory answers to each of the robotic questions that were thrown at them. They all seemed to do OK. The question that I was assigned to ask was, "What are you reading right now?" "Excuse me, Miss Johnson . . . what might you currently be reading?" I asked.

The committee received lots of varied answers. One woman said, "I just read an Amelia Bedelia book to my second-grade daughter." Another candidate said, "I just finished reading a book about how to paint with watercolors." Which was the *better* answer? Which was the *best* answer?

Again, I was confused, especially since we did not discuss that particular interview question at any point during our deliberations.

So, what if we did something different during the interviews? What if we were able to take a peek inside the souls of our candidates? What if we used our own stories to mine for our candidates' attitudes about something that we, as professionals, are burning to know?

How about this? "Excuse me, Miss Johnson, tell me a story about a child that really upset you. Tell me what you were thinking about on that challenging day. Tell me what you disliked about how things were handled or how things ended up." Better yet . . . "Miss Johnson, I'm going to have you read a story about a child who demolished a classroom because he was angry about his mother and father getting a divorce. Respond to the story by telling the committee what you would do differently or please just tell us whatever comes to your mind after reading that story."

The interview committee members could have had their own feelings about such a story and used these as a basis for structuring a philosophy governing classroom management and crisis intervention. Then, they could have seen and felt what their candidates' attitudes were about such an event.

Narrative tools can take you beyond the typical paper documents that we all use to screen and hire candidates. Maybe, just maybe, we can position ourselves to learn more about those who sit at our interview tables or who click "apply" to our on-line application systems. Maybe we can screen candidates by e-mailing them a few narratives that we would like for them to complete prior to the decision-making that goes in to whom we invite to meet later on in the hiring process.

What Is Different About This Book?

You might be thinking, "Here's just another book about hiring." This one is different, however. In a recent survey regarding the importance of attitudes and dispositions when making hiring decisions 95% of respondents noted that they are unsure about how to mine for their applicants/candidates' attitudes during their recruitment and hiring processes. Using narrative automatically opens up the floodgates for evoking so many emotions, responses, attitudes, fears, struggles, or victories from educators over time.

Preface

People have complex and independent belief systems that govern their attitudes about any topic that is dear to them. When speaking to educators about enacting the narrative process as one tool for hiring the very best educators or school staff, the number one concern for using a narrative process has to do with the amount of time it adds to the overall talent search. This is often a false assumption and will be addressed in more detail in Chapters 7 and 9, so stay tuned.

Instead, think about what you can do right now to start small. What can happen between now and the next time you meet a job candidate? This book is meant to *haunt* you into wanting to know more—much more—about your candidates with a few simple steps that can become meaningful for both you and your entire interview team or school. When educators or school staff members read the narratives included within this book, they tell me how much they can relate to the real-world stories that illustrate all of our human emotions about education and schooling. Think about the hot topics in education right now: teacher assessment, national or local learning standards, school accountability, charter schools, digital learning. What you believe about these topics forms your attitudes for working through those topics each day that you wake up and enter into your profession. This book celebrates what you go through each day while your passion for children drives you to keep returning to your beloved careers of the heart.

How This Book Will be Useful to You

This book describes a recruitment and hiring process that uses narratives that you can implement starting right now. It is easy to use and it will provide you with new, innovative results that you have never seen before out of your previous hiring methods. This book also uses many narrative examples to illustrate the narrative process in action. Use these narratives as reference tools only, however. Each narrative was created for a unique situation as defined by the school or team that was hiring a new staff member. Your narratives will look different as you work with your own team in the future. However, reading these examples will benefit you by positioning you to use them for staff discussions, professional development, or training tools. Feel free to use them as model narratives to find a way in to an issue that you are currently tackling.

This book was written for K–12 educators who sit on interview teams, school leaders, central office leaders, and higher education faculty and students who want to learn more about effectively recruiting and hiring the best school staff possible.

This book consists of nine essential chapters. Chapter 1 urges readers to delve deeper into the attitudes and dispositions of applicants and candidates that participate in talent searches. This chapter also introduces what narrative tools are and why they are exciting to use.

Chapter 2 discusses some challenges of traditional educational searches by looking at all of the typical parts and pieces, such as reviewing résumés and transcripts. This chapter doesn't denounce these screening tools. Rather, Chapter 2 places a call out to readers to consider whether there is more that we can do to uncover applicants' attitudes—especially when considering the potential power of using narratives in your talent-search process.

Chapter 3 provides research and theory supporting why narrative tools are extremely important for you and your talent-search team.

Chapter 4 and Chapter 5 help you to get all of your resources, hiring process, and human capital in order so that you can unleash the power of using narrative tools within your talent-search process.

Chapter 6 teaches you how to assess your applicants' and candidates' narrative creations or responses so you know how to extract meaning and importance from the narrative responses that you are actually receiving. This chapter helps you to align your desired responses with the attitudes that you hope will come out during your talent search.

Chapter 7 and Chapter 8 provide more real-life examples of two school districts that use narrative tools as part of their talent-search process.

Chapter 9 uncovers some common myths about using narrative tools and provides insights and advice to readers about how to effectively use narratives while avoiding any potential pitfalls. This chapter also celebrates the power of narrative tools by sharing the experiences of current narrative-tool users.

Finally, in addition to *Hiring the Best Staff for Your School,* you will find various eResources which include rubrics, templates, and guides to

Preface

assist you in your talent searches. They are available for downloading at: www.routledge.com/9781138125476.

A continued research study regarding narrative theory and hiring practices is also currently being conducted, and you can have the chance to participate in a world-wide on-line survey found at: https://docs.google.com/forms/d/1D9Lyefc3yinTgyORoI3G7_Yf_SNg8LH8KKdtzuGzXWo/viewform, or visit www.rickjetter.com or www.rjconsultants.org.

# Acknowledgments

I've always had a love for human resources administration and hiring personnel. It is fun and exciting. I met hundreds and hundreds of amazing educators over the years. I enjoyed making candidates feel comfortable and welcome whenever they came into my school or district. Meeting a future boss or interviewing in front of potential future colleagues is nerve-wracking for many people.

Listening to others is what spearheaded my love for stories and conducting research on the success that narratives could provide for knowing more about your candidates' beliefs and attitudes.

I need to thank a few groups of people and a few specific people. First, Dr. Peter Loehr, my educational leadership professor and "advisor for life," has been a true friend and expert about so much that interests me. We wrestled with ideas, brainstormed strategies, and grew our think-tank experiences and dreams for schools into real, research-based realities.

Peter sat in on my dissertation defense regarding high-stakes testing (which is still an enormous hot topic today) and narrative theory as a research platform when he asked the only question in the entire room of 30 attendees after I presented my findings: "Rick, have you ever thought about using narrative theory within the hiring process for educators?" That was almost six years ago. I liked his brainstorm so much that I decided to look into that topic a bit further. I conducted research, talked to lots of educators, and received insights into a gap in educational research that still exists today but is narrowing due to some great research work that is being written about the importance of professional attitudes and dispositions.

Dr. Suzanne Miller, my doctoral advisor and friend, was just as excited about narrative theory as I was when conducting my research years ago.

Acknowledgments

Suzanne is one of the brightest professors in the field of education today and she was instrumental in keeping my thirst for research quenched.

I would like to thank Heather Jarrow, at Routledge, for her incredible insights and excitement about *Hiring the Best Staff for Your School*, and Ruth Bennett for terrific copy-editing. Also, I'd like to thank Karen Adler for being a kind and humorous point-of-contact at Routledge and for her customer service to so many great authors.

I decided to reach out to another Eye on Education author once my manuscript was accepted by Routledge, so I got in touch with Todd Whitaker. When I first e-mailed Todd, I was a total stranger to him. I remember seeing Todd speak at a few workshops that I attended in two of my previous careers as a teacher and principal. When I connected with Todd, he provided me with some terrific input on anything that I asked him, including writing style, cover design, and upcoming book ideas. Routledge is certainly a family.

Finally, there are so many educators and interview team members who created what is included in this book. So many great teachers, principals, and friends wanted to know more about how to dig deeper and mine for candidates' attitudes and dispositions. Thank you for your insights. You are the research *within* this book. You are the ones who make stories come alive. I hope this book helps everyone who needs another tool in the toolbox for finding the highest quality school staff, and who has the best intentions, attitudes, and ignition-spark to skyrocket your institutions into even greater altitudes. We all want to hire the very best and it is possible when we add just a few sprinkles of narrative into our main recipe, which is to carry out one of the most important responsibilities in education: finding the "best" staff members during our talent searches, and then hiring the "best" because we know so much more about them now.

Meet the Author

Dr. Rick Jetter has worked in the field of education for over 17 years. He started his career as an alternative education teacher before becoming a middle school English teacher. He has held public school leadership positions as middle school assistant principal, elementary school principal, assistant superintendent, and superintendent of schools before pursuing a career of educational consulting, speaking, and conducting narrative research. Rick serves the educational community as Director of Business Development at a major educational resources company in New York State.

While completing his doctorate in learning and instruction at the State University of New York at Buffalo, Rick's research work continues to focus on using narrative theory as a tool for educational communities so that they may grow stronger in their professional capabilities and identities. Since the beginning of his research, which focused on principals' narratives and their attitudes about high-stakes testing, Rick has continued to study modern educational topics through the lens of narrative or storytelling. Rick is passionate about listening to others' stories as they illustrate many different reflections and attitudes about the powerful craft of teaching, learning, and leading. Reflections and attitudes are garnered through narrative tools and they can assist you with whom you will ultimately hire as the best staff member for your school or district.

Rick also writes across other genres including young-adult fiction, free-verse poetry, and other non-fiction books. Rick's other upcoming titles include *The Isolate /n./*, a middle grades novel about an autistic sixth-grader who struggles with agoraphobia, which will be published by Twilight Times Books. His third book, entitled *Sutures of the Mind: Unleashing the Power of Mindfulness in 30 Days While Rescuing Your Spirit,* will be published by Motivational Press.

Meet the Author

For Rick, writing is calming, creative, and fun. That's why he takes so much interest in the stories that you can tell about your experiences working with students or your craft of teaching and learning. Rick is compelled by how stories evoke emotions, frame attitudes, and unite us while we seek to add some flavor to what we see on bland paper while recruiting and hiring school staff members.

Rick is married to Jennifer and they have three children, Edward, Honora, and Ellen, as well as Rick's step-son, Timothy. Rick also has two grandsons: Dale and Emmett.

For more information about participating in future books that discuss the power of narrative theory, please visit www.rickjetter.com in order to carry out a brief, anonymous survey which will help our community of higher education faculty, narrative researchers, school leaders, and teachers learn even more about hiring practices across the globe and using the power of narrative for finding the best staff for your school. You may also contact Rick at drjetter1@gmail.com or sign up for his free newsletter on his website.

 Putting the "Best" Back Into Hiring

To all school and school district leaders, principals and superintendents, higher education faculty, teachers and teacher aides, custodians and cafeteria monitors: something is still missing from our recruitment and hiring processes when selecting the next "best" hire to work along-side you in your school or institution.

As schools and school districts across the nation engage in recruitment and hiring practices, often a typical summer-time task for hiring educators, the entire process sometimes feels like drudgery involving sifting through a long mailing list of résumés, and documents for any number of applicants. Those involved in the complicated decision-making mechanics of hiring sometimes end up filtering some of the "humanness" out of the very human business of finding the best teacher to educate our children. We all have good intentions in what we do as educators and we hope to find a candidate who will be exceedingly instrumental in providing the very best education for our schools and organizations. We hope to find that best fit, the one who comes out on top from a field of applicants that we have to somehow manage and rank. But, how do we get there and feel confident that we used as many multiple measures as we could to carry out a successful talent search?

What if, after all your hard work, you find yourself collaborating with fellow staff members who have very different attitudes and dispositions about education than you initially thought you "purchased" through your hiring process and, ultimately, after the final job offer to a candidate? So much "human" research has been presented with the claim that "nothing is more important to the overall success of a school than selecting excellent teachers and leaders" (Danielson & McGreal, 2000; Fullan, 2001;

Marzano, Pickering, & Pollock, 2001; Stronge, 2002; and Kersten, 2008). Don't get me wrong: while I agree with this statement, usually the connotation behind finding excellent teachers or the best school staff member has to do with the quality of their knowledge, skills, and abilities.

Adding an Additional Multiple Measure for Hiring the "Best"

This book puts back some of the "humanness" that is inadvertently lost from hiring practices across the nation. What if the old adage "students deserve to have the best educators" could now be transformed into the statement "students deserve to have the best educators who also have impeccable attitudes and dispositions about students, learning, assessments, and the culture of your school?" (These four SLAC creeds will be discussed later in this book.)

But, how in the world can this be accomplished? How can you measure attitudes and dispositions? And, what does the word "attitudes" really mean? How can we locate, make sense of, or even evaluate a candidate's attitudes and dispositions in some sort of standardized or scientific way? It sounds like quantifying something that can't be quantified. Can we put a price tag on love? Can we put a price tag on a new teacher being hired for a hopeful and bright long-lasting career? Maybe hiring a teacher is a $2,000,000 investment over the course of a career and you certainly don't want to spend this amount of money on someone who has poor attitudes about students, learning, achievement, or the culture of a school, along with any other educational topic or dilemma that exists in education. It is substantially important that you have some good insights about the person you desire to hire and go beyond the interview suit that was worn or the typical questions that we ask.

Can we rate the importance of someone's entire life achievements on a scale of 1–10? This is something that is immeasurable unless you establish some criteria for evaluating life and do it in a standardized way for everyone across the board. That can be hard though, and sometimes controversial.

So, how do we get to the heart of uncovering someone's attitudes and dispositions? Narratives can help. We can draw out and even seek to measure someone's true underlying attitudes to match your organization's hiring criteria through their stated and expressed beliefs, experiences, responses to, or declaration of feelings and emotions about any topic in the world by using the art and science of narrative. I will use the words "stories" and "narratives" interchangeably within this book.

Human Feelings Elicit Attitudes

We all tell stories. We love stories. We laugh at them, cry when hearing some of them, and we might even relate to or argue about something that someone is telling us through a story. We remember stories. They resonate with us. Language empowers us. Humans use metaphors to relate to one another. Stories bend us, shape us, and make us more human as we share the world with one another through our "told stories." The story-teller gets just as much out of the story exchange as the story-receiver does. It is a dialogic process for learning and reflection which is an interactive, human process (Bakhtin, 1981).

Stories draw out what we believe, who we are, and who we want to become. Stories go beyond seeking the knowledge, skills, and abilities that we all want for hiring not only the best teachers, but for hiring the best educators and school staff.

So why don't we invite storytelling into our own hiring practices when searching for excellent educators and school staff? It's human. It's reflective. And, it's easy. It can tell you a lot about a candidate that you cannot glean from an application, résumé, other application documents, or within a brief 40-60 minute interview of your candidates. And, you cannot interview everyone who has applied for a position either. That would take days. Months. Even longer.

Remember, the process outlined in this book will not discriminate against anyone in any way, nor will it insist that using narrative theory models for interviewing candidates should be the only deciding factor for whom you ultimately hire. Rather, it will seek to separate potentially poor candidates from the potentially quality candidates who exhibit incredible attitudes and dispositions that *match* your organization's goals, beliefs, and focus.

As you read this book, I'd like for you to remember two main themes as I outline a process that can work for your school or district:

1. We need to have a window into the souls of the professionals who work in educational settings. Without it, we take a gamble on attitudes that only become even more "hardened" over time. Knowledge can be explored, skills can be taught, and abilities can be practiced. Attitudes can't be taught. Attitudes can also be hard to remediate.
2. This book describes a process that can work in your organization, small or large. If stakeholders from your organization are not involved, you will see no benefit to using, authoring, and assessing narratives or the attitudes of your candidates.

Proven Success

While there is limited research in the field for using narrative theory models within hiring processes, some work has been done in New York State and is reported in this book when describing various school districts—which are protected by pseudonyms so information does not lead to an identification of specific employees by releasing private personnel information.

In order to provide further insights into the process of using narratives and how they can be applied to a school district recruiting or hiring process, two school districts, given the pseudonyms of the Elm Grove Central School District and the Gardenville City School District, illustrate how a narrative process unfolds in two different demographic situations, in two different sized districts, and fostered in schools that have different hiring needs.

Data has been extracted from these school districts which determine a significant qualitative correlation between the success rates on narrative models and the success of a candidate in his or her new position.

Have fun reading the narratives within this book as they offer a lot of scenarios that you might be thinking about or have experienced, yourself, as a school professional.

What if candidates were to create or respond to narratives on various relevant educational topics that "measured" the quality of their attitudes and dispositions in a manner that matched the hiring criteria set by your schools? What if the hiring process of those believed to be quality candidates—in terms of traditional knowledge, skills, and abilities—could add a dose of attitudinal analysis for you and your hiring committees?

That would ultimately lead to better hiring decisions, happier employees, increased student achievement, and more staff support for the school goals that you wish to implement. Narrative theory not only adds flavor to your hiring palate but also becomes a science, something that can actually be measured.

What Does the Word "Best" Really Mean?

It is semantics, I guess, but let's break it down. My children call me the "world's *greatest* dad" on Father's Day. Isn't "great" better than "good," especially when we think about Jim Collins' book, *Good to great: Why some companies make the leap . . . and others don't?* So, isn't "best" better than "better?" If I was the "world's *best* dad," would that mean more to the dad? I think it would. "World's *better* dad" just doesn't sound too *good*. I mean, "sound too *great*."

When you think about hiring the "best" school staff, it is important for you to think about what "best" really means. It is not a fancy word used in the title of the book simply to sell more books. Instead, think about these three characteristics of "best" when you read all of the narratives within this book:

1. Your job is to find the "best" hire, not the "better" hire.
2. The word "best" will now mean that you are looking at *attitudes and dispositions* in addition to the knowledge, skills, and abilities of your job applicants/candidates.
3. The word "best" also means that whomever you hire will also be the "best" fit for your school or district. I don't believe in creating robots in your school where everyone must think the same about a topic or issue, but let's face it: sometimes we think about people as not being the "best" fit for our organizations and sometimes it's too late to remediate someone's attitudes about something that comes from inside them.

Let's start the process by first identifying some of the challenges of traditional talent searches in order to understand how narrative tools, now more than ever, are so important during the recruitment, screening, and interviewing process of schools and districts. Attitudes can be uncovered very easily if you follow the simple eight-step process outlined below:

1. Assemble a talent search team.
2. Determine how you will use powerful, narrative tools.
3. Align those tools with specific attitudes that you wish to glean from your candidates.
4. Implement the four SLAC creeds (students, learning, achievement, and culture) as a guide for authoring your narrative tools.
5. Select a writer from your school, district, or team who will write the actual narratives to be used.
6. Craft your narratives and gather responses.
7. Assess your responses.
8. Determine next steps by using your new information as an additional multiple measure for deciding your BEST hire!

References

Bakhtin, M. M. (1981). *The dialogic imagination: 4 Essays by M. M. Bakhtin, M. Holquist (ed.).* Austin: University of Texas Press.
Collins, J. (2001). *Good to great: Why some companies make the leap . . . and others don't.* New York: HarperCollins.
Danielson, C., & McGreal, T. (2000). *Teacher evaluation to enhance professional practice.* Alexandria, VA: Association for Supervision and Curriculum Development.
Fullan, M. (2001). *Leading in a culture of change.* San Francisco: Jossey-Bass.
Kersten, T. (2008). Teacher hiring practices: Illinois principals' perspectives. *The Educational Forum, 72,* 355–368.
Marzano, R., Pickering, D., & Pollock, J. (2001). *Classroom instruction that works.* Alexandria, VA: Association for Supervision and Curriculum Development.
Stronge, J. (2002). *Qualities of effective teachers.* Alexandria, VA: Association for Supervision and Curriculum Development.

Some Challenges With Traditional Educational Talent Searches

One of the biggest challenges in hiring school employees is that there is so much variance. It is sometimes an inconsistent process, or unintentional rather than intentional. In some cases, it is illegal or not equal. There might not even be any documentation to prove that the process was really open to all applicants—especially when the decisions are made to invite only a small number of candidates to an interview. You may set up criteria that the candidates need to meet. You might not. You might have a series of elaborate forms that scale who should be invited to an interview and who does not make the cut. You might hide these documents in your office filing cabinet and you might not share your rating scales with anyone outside of the hiring team. Maybe you follow a strong posting process that would enable many candidates to apply for a position. Maybe you don't.

Think back to your last job recruitment attempt: You are up to your ears with looking at candidates' grade-point averages, reading reference letters, and thinking about "whom you might like." But, really, you find that it is extremely difficult to find out as much as you can about a candidate. You might know some candidates who have applied—even personally . . . a friend . . . former employee . . . acquaintances . . . but those are your only leads besides who the candidates are on paper.

You have no idea about the person behind the paper. Hours are spent deciphering. But, you really do not know anything about what attitudes you expect from a candidate and what your organization believes in. The problem is that you cannot extract something so human, such as attitudes or dispositions from paper. You can try, but it is extremely difficult. You might read the candidate's professional statement regarding their teaching philosophy which only ends up looking like something you already read.

Blurry lines exist because all people want to look good on paper. After all, that is usually how they enter into the interview process unless you are doing something ego-centric, such as granting an interview to your neighbor's brother or hiring your aunt.

Now, picture this: you need to hire a Grade 9 math teacher. Your school district has an electronic application warehouse. You post the position. People apply by clicking a few computer buttons. They upload their résumé and other "stuff." You wait for the posting deadline to end. Then, you find out that 193 applicants are interested in becoming the next new addition to your faculty!

You might feel like pulling your hair out. Now, compound that number into an even higher applicant number, especially if the economy is poor and people are looking for work, not to mention the fact that you might be working in a school district is surrounded by teacher training colleges and universities. The environmental factors can add to your time reviewing applications, which then becomes a night-time nightmare, a homework load that is heavier than your own high-school junior.

It is important to stress one major point before we go any further. I am not advocating the elimination of traditional documents used in the application process; I am advocating supplementing the use of narratives into your pre-screening process so that you have the ability to get to the heart of others' hearts before you invite them to an interview. After all, when you look at the traditional types of forms and documents used for screening applicants (outlined in the next section), you will be able to see how none of these types of application materials get to what you are really looking for: insight into the attitudes and dispositions of candidates and ways of matching them to your organization's core beliefs about teaching, learning, best practices, and the overall care of your students.

One hundred teachers and school district officials in New York State were surveyed about their hiring tools and processes and asked them to rank the following application documents according to the importance of screening applicants for a potential first interview. These documents or hiring tools consisted of:

- the résumé
- the application
- college transcripts

- state certification documents
- letters of reference
- the cover letter
- the portfolio

I will share the results with you in the next section, but keep one thing in mind: the majority of schools and school districts believe that the job interview is one of the most important factors in determining hiring potentiality because it is face-to-face. But, the problem with interviews is that many schools do not ask questions pertaining to the attitudes and dispositions of their candidates. There are some books written about dispositions, but few, if any, invest in the art of designing and utilizing narratives.

Traditional Application Documents

As stated earlier, the information presented below was gathered from a 2010–2013 survey on hiring practices in K–12 schools and school districts across the nation. Teachers, school leaders, and district-level school leaders participated in the survey. This book does not devalue the following topics as you carry out your talent search; rather, this book promotes adding another multiple measure for you to mine for attitudes.

The Résumé

We love the résumé. We really do. And, we need it as a method for a quick review of a candidate's experiences—a sort of summary for the employer. But, it has its flaws even though over 43% of educators thought that the résumé was among the top instruments to use for determining a hiring decision.

Let's analyze one type of résumé. Notice Joan's (a pseudonym) résumé in Table 2.1. Joan was a candidate at the Elm Grove Central School District (which we will talk more about in Chapter 7) for a Grade 8 ELA teaching position and as you look at this document, think about what might make Joan stand out from any other candidate that was in the running at the Elm Grove Central School District.

Table 2.1

	JOAN TRAVERSE
	411 Clipping Ave.
	Pine Hills, NY 11150
	273–1177 (home)
	271–0110 (cell phone)
CERTIFICATION	**New York State Teacher Certification**
	Permanent, Secondary English (7–12), Sept. 1991
EDUCATION	**Center State University**
	Master of Science in English Education, Aug. 1993
	Overall GPA: 4.0/4.0
	Center State University
	Teacher Certification Program, May 1991
	Overall GPA: 3.9/4.0
	North Town University
	Bachelor of Arts in English, May 1990
	Major GPA: 3.8/4.0
PROFESSIONAL EXPERIENCE	**South City School District**
	English/Language Arts Teacher, Long-Term Substitute
	October 1991–December 1991
	• Taught eighth-grade English to a team of 115 students—which included a population of gifted and talented students, at-risk students, and severely handicapped students.
	• Utilized differentiated instructional strategies by using special area course content—as a means for promoting interdisciplinary instructional links.
	• Used the New York State Learning Standards as a foundation for developing interdisciplinary reading and writing programs in science and social studies.
STUDENT TEACHING	**Windgate Middle School**
	English/Language Arts Teacher, Grade 7
	January 1991–March 1991
	• Facilitated writing across the content areas, concerning specialized science topics, such as nuclear energy and waste management.

	• Carried out guided reading using secondary book clubs. • Used mini-book circles for differentiating comprehension tasks. **Falls Ridge High School** *English/Language Arts Teacher, Grade 12* March 1991–May 1991 • Used drama techniques for acting out setting and characters within novel studies. • Taught AP English to a class of 13 seniors. • Sponsored the senior writing club which focused on fiction writing and poetry.
REFERENCES	• Furnished upon request.

So, what is the problem here? Well, maybe it is too generic? Maybe it is too boring? Maybe the formatting is perfect? Maybe the spelling is flawless and the layout is superb? It looks like Joan has some experience too. Maybe we can also gain some insight into her age—based on the years she went to college—OOPS! No, we shouldn't look at that, but we, unfortunately, can't help but to look at it because we are human. Maybe, we are pleased with Joan's Grade Point Average, but maybe other résumés have that same GPA (I'll get to the topic of college transcripts later).

The problem with the résumé is that after reviewing each nook and cranny, you are still left with no insights about the attitudes and dispositions of the applicant. That's the challenge. And, little to no research examines the quality of a résumé as a determinant for success as a school employee. See, the problem is that résumés start to look the same. We might only discern differences in experiences and experience-based durations and maybe even discount "the rookie" (just out of college) because we are living in a school district buyer's market—a time where we have enormous numbers of applicants for only a few vacant jobs each year.

School districts are in control of whom to interview and whom to ultimately hire. But, there is little to no creativity in the area of testing a candidate's inherent attitudes about education and children. Most of all, it takes more time than the usual practices that school districts use. I will discuss this further in Chapter 7 because while utilizing narratives within your recruitment and hiring process does take more time, it isn't going to throw your schedule overboard and leave you with an e-mail inbox that keeps you up all night because you are now behind in everything else that you needed to accomplish. Remember this, however, one of *the* most important things that you can do as a school leader or teacher is to be part of leading a hiring process that results in hiring the very best staff member for your students.

One wouldn't go to a car dealer and buy a Corvette off the showroom floor just because it looked good. But, if finding the safest car for my three children is priority number one for me, the Corvette just won't work for me. Résumés typically look good. Sure, you come across some spelling errors now and again, but those types of errors should not be an exclusionary method used for weeding out candidates—perhaps even quality candidates who slipped on the keyboard. All of those "rules" about not interviewing someone because they typed a "b" instead of a "d" in the word "leadership" won't tell you a lot about the heart and soul of your candidates. Everyone is human and should someone be disqualified because of a typo?

Sure, there are hiring officials who find spelling errors to be inexcusable, just as I might exclude a showroom car because of a deflated tire. They perceive the candidate as sloppy, lazy, or inattentive to the tiniest details—again, all of these speculations do not get to the heart of what you should really be looking for in your applicants: attitudes. So, at best, the résumé is a concise document from which to get a ton of information about a candidate which may or may not help you to decide whom to interview.

The Application

The paper application for formally applying to a school or school district is cumbersome, but one can also understand its place for establishing equal employment opportunities (EOE) and a legal process for school districts to canvass and recruit educational candidates. Most school district officials actually hate their formal application document, because it replicates the information from the résumé. Fewer than 3% of educators thought that the application document was among the top instruments to use for determining a hiring decision; yet, the application is one of the most tedious documents to fill out and candidates are often excluded when they fail to fill it out. Maybe this requirement has more to do with conforming to the requests of the employer rather than anything else.

For schools that do not have an on-line application system, paper applications usually only regurgitate the same information that a résumé usually already has. These application documents are often long-winded asking questions such as where candidates went to high school and the address of that school. At that point, a candidate might be thinking . . . "Well, I couldn't have gotten my B.A. at the university that I attended if I hadn't graduated from high school, or passed the General Educational Development (GED) tests . . . and I couldn't have gotten a Master of Education (M.S. Ed) if I hadn't had my undergraduate degree."

Anyway, paper applications formalize the application process. But, these also exist as a disqualifier, as I stated above. If one does not fill the application out, one might be excluded from going any further in the hiring process. Any one missing document that is requested of a candidate by a prospective employer will disqualify that candidate, often automatically, and become labeled as an "incomplete" application. It's like not turning in a homework assignment. A few human resources officials compile tables with checkmarks on who submitted what and who will not receive any credit for their incomplete assignment.

School districts often come across applications that say "see résumé" and this infuriates some hiring personnel because, just like the résumé with spelling mistakes, this suggests laziness on the candidate's part. Is this fair? Maybe not—perhaps you will be excluding a candidate who really has the attitudes that your school is looking for. You want the best candidate, don't you? Maybe we sometimes sweat the small stuff.

There is typically a section on an application form that asks for a "candidate's statement" or "philosophy of education." Sometimes there are essay questions that really only receive responses that demonstrate knowledge, skills, or generic beliefs. Since these are treated as writing samples similar to having an open-book test, we often fail to use these paragraphs for deeper analysis or as a multiple measure for the final consideration in hiring the best candidate. Looking at the writing samples for correctness of expression only repeats the problems discussed earlier: we set up processes that only serve to exclude candidates, rather than using these tools for something more. You might be left with great statements or paragraphs from all of your candidates and this leaves you with lengthy term-papers that might all receive a grade "A." You have no way to rate, evaluate, or assess these written statements because they might not be truly important to you.

College Transcripts

Approximately 33% of educators thought that college transcripts were among the top instruments to use for determining a hiring decision. That is a large percentage. This is the document that many people scrutinize to find out if a candidate is intelligent. But, are you getting anything from scrutinizing transcripts?

Two math teacher applicants who applied to the Gardenville City School District (which we will talk more about in Chapter 8) can be analyzed through the lens of their master's degree transcripts. Remember, this chapter focuses on the challenges of hiring, and it aims to establish the need to canvass candidates by using new models of thought and theory in order to become holistically sound professionals with a tool belt for extracting "humanness" through our talent search.

Alex and Sarah (pseudonyms) attended college together and were in the same cohort for their mathematics education degree. Therefore, they took the same classes together at the same time. Before you take a look at these two transcript summaries, think about your own educational experiences. Did you have trouble with something? Did you struggle in a class that you hated? Did you meet a teacher or professor that you didn't like? Now, notice where your eyes might wander when you read Table 2.2.

Did Sarah's B+ stick out like a sore thumb? We see what appears to be a perfect candidate in Alex (4.0/4.0) and someone who is good (Sarah), but maybe not totally "perfect" on paper. Would Alex have a leg up on Sarah because of a 12% difference in GPA? Does a B+ on Sarah's transcript disqualify her in our minds even though we might still interview her? Unfortunately, maybe. Colleges and universities usually have a minimum grade cutoff within their majors. Receiving anything below a "B" has now become the cutoff score for getting credit for a course. Student teaching is often denoted as pass or fail. So, that won't tell you much about your candidates.

Table 2.2

Traditional College
Transcript Summary for: Alex Roberts
Degree Awarded: M.S. Ed.
Department: Mathematics Education
S= Satisfactory

Date	Dept	Course	Type	Title	Level	Credits	Grade
9/1998	MED	635	SEM	ELEMENTARY MATHEMATICS INSTRUCTION	GRA GR	3.00	A
9/1998	MED	623	SEM	ALGEBRAIC PROBLEM SOLVING	GRA GR	3.00	A
1/1999	MED	669	SEM	TECHNIQUES IN INSTRUCTION	GRA GR	3.00	A
1/1999	MED	697	LAB	RESEARCH IN MATHEMATICS INSTRUCTION	GRA GR	3.00	A
9/1999	MED	625	SEM	APPLICATIONS AND DIMENSIONS	GRA GR	3.00	A
9/1999	MED	695	LAB	EVALUATION AND ASSESSMENT	GRA GR	3.00	A

Total Credit Hours: 35   GPA: 4.0/4.0
Degree Requirements Met: December 11, 1999
Degree Conferral Date: January 8, 2000

(continued)

Table 2.2 (continued)

Traditional College
Transcript Summary for: Sarah Scotlin
Degree Awarded: M.S. Ed.
Department: Mathematics Education
S= Satisfactory

Date	Dept	Num	Type		Title		Grade Type	Grade	Credits	Grade
9/1998	MED	635	SEM		ELEMENTARY MATHEMATICS INSTRUCTION		GRA	GR	3.00	A–
9/1998	MED	623	SEM		ALGEBRAIC PROBLEM SOLVING		GRA	GR	3.00	A
1/1999	MED	669	SEM	A	TECHNIQUES IN INSTRUCTION		GRA	GR	3.00	A
1/1999	MED	697	LAB		RESEARCH IN MATHEMATICS INSTRUCTION		GRA	GR	3.00	A
9/1999	MED	625	SEM		APPLICATIONS AND DIMENSIONS		GRA	GR	3.00	A
9/1999	MED	695	LAB		EVALUATION AND ASSESSMENT		GRA	GR	3.00	A

Total Credit Hours: 35   GPA: 3.88/4.0
Degree Requirements Met: December 11, 1999
Degree Conferral Date: January 8, 2000

Do we all have strengths/weaknesses or likes/dislikes? Might a Spanish teacher struggle in calculus class? These factors are not predictors of quality teachers with quality attitudes who might be the best fit for your organization.

No research concludes that a GPA of 4.0/4.0 produces a more successful teacher than one who has a 3.88/4.0. What about going down to a 3.5/4.0 or a 3.1? Again, there is no research regarding these differentials. Sometimes we get hung up on numbers when trying to find the most perfect candidate, but this gambling may mean disposing of a high quality candidate.

Candidates with 4.0/4.0 GPAs are more attractive on paper because they followed the rules of formal schooling and/or appeared to excel in everything that they did. Maybe they just followed the institutional rules and better navigated the educational discourse that was presented to them. To us, we perceive greatness through their "achieved" numbers. What if a 3.1/4.0 GPA candidate has the attitudes and dispositions that you are looking for in your school and they are just as talented and "smart" as the next person? Well, you may have just passed up a great addition to your staff.

Certifications

Certifications are simply a prerequisite to fulfill the fact that staff are considered to be "highly qualified" under the "No Child Left Behind" (NCLB) Act. Teacher candidates must receive state certification in order to be considered "highly qualified" even though some schools of thought see this as a barrier to recruiting exceptional teachers. Nevertheless, school districts demand that these be a prerequisite to the actual hiring of a candidate even though the attitudes of candidates vary even when they are certified to teach in a particular state. Certifications only tell us one thing: that a course of study was completed in education and guidelines were followed to become "certified," often requiring hefty fees for taking tests. I've met some terrific test-takers who had strange philosophies about how to manage a classroom or discipline a student.

In order to become "certified," candidates must pass state tests within their content area—which include writing samples and multiple choice questions, questions, mind you, that do not elicit the attitudes of educational employees. The pass rate ranges for these tests are often quite generous and they give potential employers no insights into the attitudes of these individuals since they do not even report the areas of deficiencies on the test items that were scored.

In fact, there are a *huge* number of "mean" people who pass these tests—educators who have terrible attitudes about children, systems of education, parents, or educational philosophies—and, unfortunately, slide past interview teams and become employed. This is exactly the kind of situation that narrative theory can analyze in any school system. It can delve very deep and get to the root of someone's beliefs.

Being "certified" on paper does not make an applicant the best professional to care for and educate children.

What does a sheet of paper like this really tell you? Practically nothing. Just under 2% of educators thought that providing a copy of a candidate's certification was among the top instruments to use for determining a hiring decision—especially because these certifications have tiers for renewal and most are provided with an initial or provisional certification status until further work experience and education are completed over time. Certification, then, is perceived as being, only a lens into the amount of schooling completed by a candidate and if a candidate met the state requirements by formally filing for their certification. Most importantly, school districts use state search engines to check the status of certification filing and fingerprints, so school officials really do not need a copy of a certification because it doesn't tell them much about a candidate. Of course, we need proof of certification, but this category is really more about school districts who feel they should still be using paper and files versus those who are now doing everything digitally.

For your organization, a certified candidate could have wonderful attitudes about their craft, or not. You have no idea if that person's attitudes about learning, thoughts about professional development or self-reflection, beliefs about extracurricular activities for children, or feelings about discipline philosophies will match those of your organization or match the direction that your school or school district is heading towards when it comes to carrying out new initiatives, programs, or policies. Any applicant might just be one of the certified "ghosts" that apply to your school and who have all of their paperwork in order.

Letters of Reference (a.k.a. The Placement Folder)

Letters of reference often all look the same. About 15% of educators thought that letters of reference were among the top instruments to use for determining a hiring decision. Reference checks are more powerful through personal phone calls.

Letters of reference can backfire. Letters that are gleaming or just generically supporting a candidate on paper can represent the old "we will write a good letter so we can get rid of this person" mentality. Certainly, this is not ethical and obviously, we hesitate to say anything "bad" about a candidate for fear that we will be guilty of muddying the talent search process. Late night phone calls to our colleagues usually clean up unanswered questions, but situations that boost particular applicants happen all of the time and there is more "black-balling" going on in our nation than we can possibly fathom. About a dozen school superintendents told me stories about job candidates that they checked out by talking to a colleague or friend behind the scenes.

References should be documented by the caller. Questions should be meaningful and purposeful. The reality to all of this is that there are lots of undocumented references or phone calls that take place privately. Sometimes this is good. Sometimes it isn't. If we learn something disturbing about a candidate, that is a good thing. If employers have their own hang-ups and bash a candidate for not fitting in or doing well because of a personality conflict, that is when decisions might become unfair. You cannot truly discount candidates who were unsuccessful somewhere else because everything is situational. But, talent searches do this all the time. Any red check mark in anyone's career history often leads them to the "no" pile. What you are trying to do, however, is match a candidate's attitudes with your organization's attitudes. A poor "paper candidate" might be your diamond-in-the-rough candidate, and that is one of the major problems with hiring. I mentioned this earlier. Take a teacher who is trying to set thoughtful homework policies that the other teachers in the school disagree with and they then become adversaries. That makes for a tough professional relationship with colleagues there, but this person could be the next new addition to your staff because maybe they are the best!

What about a superintendent who was trying to challenge the status quo on contract negotiations, but the board of education cut him or her loose because of the treacherous relationship between the unions which resulted from a disagreeable negotiation process? Again, everything is situational. But, some letters of reference might try to get rid of these "pushing-the-status-quo" leaders. There may be unemployed candidates who are just as good for your students and staff as those who are currently employed and simply desire to move around to another district for more money or prestige.

So, getting back to letter writing, there is absolutely no scientific way to judge which reference letter will support a successfully hired candidate. Neither is there any research about writing successful letters or research that uncovers a correlation between a hired candidate and the quality of their reference letters. Typically, the better the letter of reference writer is, the better the candidate appears. What we are judging is the craft of the reference writer, not the craft of the candidate or his or her attitudes and dispositions.

The Cover Letter

A candidate sends his or her résumé to you, demonstrates certification, finds a few people to write letters of reference for him or her, and encloses transcripts for your review. All of this is packaged up by the first page of this hefty packet—the cover letter.

The application process is sometimes a formality with cover letters ranking at the bottom of what professionals value. Only 1.5% of educators thought that the cover letter was among the top instruments to use for determining a hiring decision or learning something meaningful about the candidate.

Most applications include a cover letter explaining an applicant's reasons for wanting the position. Sure, we can glean some demonstration of writing competence and we can discern the differences in attention to details if one cover letter has grammatical and spelling mistakes and another is flawless. But, remember, we discussed typos earlier.

Some cover letters are exceedingly long and some are short. The long ones sometimes detail how much time and effort they put in to convincing you that they are the best-suited candidate for your job. But, again, the letter is a professional introduction, a handshake, a first impression because it bundles up a person's career in a sheet of paper.

65 out of 70 school superintendents informed me that they rarely see any content within a cover letter that elicits insight into a candidate's feelings, hot topics, or attitudes about education today. So, the cover letter is just another formality.

The Portfolio

The portfolio is perceived as a glorified photo album and only 2% of educators thought that the portfolio was among the top instruments to use for determining a hiring decision. The portfolio may include some really nice documents such as photographs, lesson plans, and written reflections that try to demonstrate the achievements of a candidate. But, the only thing that a portfolio really demonstrates is scrap-booking talent, neat organization of papers or "stuff," a tidy use of the glue stick to make this "creative thing" come alive. Some people have creative layout abilities, but this tells you nothing about the quality of the candidate other than demonstrating organizational skills and some creativity. Many carry a lavish portfolio to interviews, when the interview teams really want to focus on the person not the papers.

You see some candidates bring in their "luggage on wheels" to a job interview. They have binders with sample lesson plans, pictures upon pictures, student work samples, and all of the things that either make the interview team wonder when they will have time to look at all 1,000 pages or where they can get such nice luggage. There are also lots of candidates who bring their digital portfolio on a USB drive or CD-ROM to the interview, but one principal to whom I spoke leveled with me that he throws those things out because there isn't sufficient time to have the whole committee sit and review such lengthy files.

Hard copy portfolios get passed around the interview table. Some interviewers look at them and some glance at them as a polite gesture. You might see a candidate refer to his or her portfolio throughout the entire interview—a visual crutch to help remedy nervousness and answer questions. So, the candidate looks at their beautiful binder which motivates them to remember that they are a hardworking teacher even if they have attitudes about educational topics that might clash with your organization's philosophies. What the portfolio neglects to entertain is what exactly makes a candidate a "good teacher" or a "good fit" for a school district? Portfolios have no measures for gleaning the potential attitudes of prospective candidates.

You might see some smiling photos, but even the crabby teachers will fake a few seconds for a photo opportunity around kids. And, very few interview teams use the portfolio in making a final decision unless two candidates are neck and neck.

Picture this: "We like these two teacher applicant finalists, but we cannot make up our mind. So, let's give it to the better scrapbooker," said one school superintendent, joking around with me.

The Interview

This is the category that is most controversial. The results of over 200 educators who provided insights about their own core values for conducting talent searches lead us to a thorough discussion about the interview. Of the survey respondents, 72% stated that the interview was the most important qualifier for making a hiring decision. The work experience/track record of a candidate was the most important factor for 10% of respondents, and the remaining 10% of those surveyed identified the fact that their new hires were known entities around their schools or school districts. What this meant for some respondents was that a substitute teacher who was frequently called to work and who appeared to fit in and do a good job was considered to be their next hire. Another qualitative example was that the perception of internal candidates who "moved up the ranks" from teacher to administrator or teacher aide to teacher were the ones who would most likely be hired because they worked hard and were "next in line."

Our general idea or perception of what we think "good work" is, becomes a major challenge within hiring decision-making. But, what happens when we hire someone and they become one of the most difficult staff members to coach or lead? We then think, "Boy, I wish I'd known more about this person's attitudes before I hired this teacher."

So, 72% of educators believe that the interview will get to the "meat and potatoes" of selecting a quality candidate. They have the gut instinct to hire the best. They can just feel it. They get out their typical interview questions, sit on a committee, and then discuss who they like and don't like.

Some 98% of educators confirmed that when they interview or when they are interviewed, they rarely ask or receive questions that elicit a look into attitudes or dispositions. These same 98% of educators do not use stories or narratives as a tool for uncovering applicants' attitudes.

What Does That Question Really Search For?

We can ask anything that we want during an interview. Well, almost anything except the illegal stuff, such as: "Tell me about your kids?" or "How old did you say you were?" or "Didn't we used to date in high school?" or "I know you will fit in perfectly at our Jesuit institution, right?"

The survey respondents identified several types of questions that they ask during their interviews. These have been given categorical descriptors in order to better understand how schools are very similar in what they ask candidates:

1. **Getting-to-know-you opening questions** (a.k.a. the ice-breaker questions): These are the "welcome to our interview" questions which are all nice to use, but they will not do anything other than create an entry way for the interviewee into the interview. While these questions do not have much relevance to uncovering attitudes about a candidate, 95% of educators remember asking or being asked questions that break the ice or provide an entry way for an interviewee to feel comfortable in front of the interview team. These include: "Please talk about your experience and what brings you to our school for an interview?" "Why are you the best teacher for our school based on your education and preparation?" "What have you been working on in your current job that we will be interested in at our school?" or the most commonly hated question: "Please tell us about yourself."

2. **Demonstration of skills questions**: These are the questions that ask about a specific skill that teachers or staff members should have. These questions are meant to uncover the knowledge or skills of a candidate, and 82% of the educators who responded to a hiring survey remember asking or being asked questions such as: "What do you do to differentiate instruction?" "What can you tell us about your

guided reading practices?" "What do you do about bullying in the classroom?" "How would you lead a vision at our school?" "What technology do you use in the classroom?" "When you are managing the cafeteria, what do you do to control student misbehavior?"

Any other content-specific question is fair game within this section. Any other skill-based question for school leaders, cafeteria monitors, etc. will fall into this type of technical understanding category and this section does not uncover any attitudes about the topics that you are really dying to know more about.

3. **Scenario questions**: These are the questions that test the interviewee's judgment or quick reaction to a situation. They do not necessarily uncover attitudes about a situation, but these are the questions that do the most to mine for the attitudes and dispositions of a candidate. Unfortunately, only 28% of educators who responded to a hiring practices survey remember asking or being asked questions that pose some sort of a scenario. Such questions may also have limited usefulness because these schools might not have an *intentional* way to gauge the interviewees' responses by using any type of rating scale, rubric, or behavioral chart.

These questions, when asked, provide insights into student situations, such as: "What would you do if a student went into anaphylactic shock?" "What would you do if two students got into a fist fight in the cafeteria?" "What would you do if an angry parent confronted a teacher in the hallway?" Again, these questions do not necessarily uncover attitudes, but only serve to uncover some basic understanding of policies, procedures, ways to resolve conflict, or knowing something about a candidate's quick-thinking, gut instinct.

4. **Future goals questions**: These questions only demonstrate one of two things. Either a candidate continues to carry out professional development activities, additional college or university degrees, etc., or they don't. Then, it gives the interview team some insight into what the interviewee is interested in as they learn more about an interviewee's specific topic or area of interest.

Only 18% of educators remember asking or being asked questions that uncover an interviewee's plan or quest for further knowledge. Some questions within this category might simply ask, "What are you doing within your own professional development?" "What are you currently reading?" "What training are you pursuing?" "What do you feel you need to know more about for your career?" When asking these questions, however, the interview team might find some disappointment if the interviewee explains something that interests them, but it does not necessarily interest the interview team. So, it is a bit closed-ended in its intent and yet, again, it does not uncover anything about attitudes except that one candidate might be more driven than the next regarding something that may or may not interest the committee.

5. **School district processes questions**: These types of questions sometimes only test what an interviewee might already know about processes or procedures—either within the school culture that they are interviewing in or generalized procedures that might apply to most school contexts. Furthermore, these types of questions test an interviewee's resourcefulness on getting the correct answers about procedures even if they do not already know what those are. These types of questions were asked the least because most recruiters know that candidates might not know everything about their school or district and only 8% of educators remember asking or being asked questions that had to do with processes, such as "What process would you set up for establishing staff development opportunities for our district nurses?" "Talk about your process for communicating the school district budget to community members." "What information would you need before making a decision about a student suspension?"

Again, these types of questions help the interview team to think about how an interviewee will solve problems, be resourceful in getting the answers that will help to make the best-informed decision about an issue, or be equipped to cite policy to support decision-making—none of which get to the heart of interviewees' attitudes about the organization's deepest desires when hiring personnel.

6. **A call for candidates to ask questions**: Allowing candidates to ask questions is generally seen as a courtesy; therefore, over 98% of educators remember inviting or being invited to ask questions.

A candidate's question might help the committee gain some insight into their attitudes about a topic, but only if the interviewee is cognizant enough to use this opportunity to demonstrate some of his or her attitudes about specific educational topics. If this happens, the interview team must also be able to identify that this is consciously being done and that a demonstration of attitudes and dispositions is also sought by the interview team in the first place.

Here is an example: let's say that both the interviewee and the interview team know and understand that attitudes are important when hiring a candidate. If the interviewee asks a question, such as "What do you feel are some best practices in your school district for addressing the idea that students should regularly receive feedback about their progress in class?" What will the response be from the interview team?

After the interview team answers that question, the interviewee can go into what his or her beliefs are and be able to demonstrate the positive and powerful attitudes and dispositions that he or she might have when it comes to conferencing with students, establishing reading and writing goals for students, and monitoring what students can and cannot do as they get students to articulate and track their own progress, responsively, on their own. This, then, would be a "way in" to having discussions with the interview team about the attitudes that teachers should have about their students' progress.

Before using narrative tools, an interview team will need to define what the proper attitudes and beliefs are for teachers and school staff regarding students and educational issues. The process for establishing the criteria to mine candidates' attitudes and dispositions during the hiring process will be outlined in Chapter 4.

The research behind narrative theory can be found in the next chapter, but if research and literature reviews make you sick to your stomach or remind you of haunting thoughts about your previous graduate work, skip Chapter 3 and move on to Chapter 4. Whatever you decide, Chapter 3 sets the table for appreciating narrative theory and recognizing its purposefulness in the educational arena.

Why Narratives?

Why? Because narratives can assist you with attitude analysis. Plus, who wouldn't want to have some sort of insight into the attitudes and dispositions of future school staff members? This chapter will identify some of the theory behind narratives or storytelling and equip you to understand how narrative tools can be used to promote forward thinking, the assessment of attitudes, and self-reflection and refraction of the "self" in relation to "others."

A teacher may have the knowledge or skills to design a lesson plan, carry out that lesson plan, or administer a defibrillator machine during an emergency, but it is the essence of the individual's attitudes or dispositions that will allow him or her to outlast any other teacher or educator in practice. Your best hires will defeat career burn-out, be more open to self-diagnosis, and be able to adapt to changes without seeking negative conflict.

Narratives "Counting" as Research

Whether stories are gathered from students, teachers, or other professionals, everyone truly has a "story" to tell. Stories can be a collection of ongoing experiences or insights from human beings and they can offer glimpses into identity—changing patterns that are always fluidly "in the making" over time, as well. Polkinghorne (1988) characterizes narrative-telling as a "human science," which has intrigued many scholars in the fields of sociology and psychology, but storytelling has also made its way into the educational arena. Qualitative researchers have looked carefully at the role of using narratives and storytelling as a compelling and valid way to reveal a different type of "human data" that these research methods can gather, as

Why Narratives?

narratives find their way into the world of educating children (Perl et al., 2007, p. 306).

Altman (2008) proposes that "narratives [or stories] occupy the bulk of sacred texts, insomuch that when there is no narrative, there is no history" (p. 1), nor is there a story behind the human. Narratives are not meant to capture plot lines only. A new way of thinking about narratives in research would be to recognize a story's "action and character so representing a rise and fall, loss or recovery, or desire and acquisition can be relative to knowing more about the actors on a stage of ongoing life events" (Altman, 2008, pp. 11–12). Education is constantly changing. Controversial political issues like standardized testing or the Common Core State Standards dominate news headlines. Utilizing narratives will get you to the hearts of your candidates within a talent search so that you can hire the very best.

Fashioning a text, according to Zinsser's (1987) focus on memoir writing, is what matters most when capturing "time and remembrance through an experience of writing." This can become even more powerful than a person's story being "lived" at a certain point in time or history (p. 27). Simply put, writing evokes emotion and materializes experience beyond a fixed entity in time. Educators live in and identify with the culture that surrounds them—whether it reflects their beliefs, identities, or desires. A school culture is not a fixed entity, and all educators have stories to tell about their worlds.

Stories can bring about an essential way of knowing the world or "narrativizing experiences" according to the work of Bruner (1986, 1990). Through narrative, we are trying to look closely, pay attention, and be the "bricoleurs of our experiences so that the reader has a door to open and walk through" (Schaafsma & Vinz, 2007, p. 277). Researchers who use narratives to inquire and to present their research understand that "stories are filled with languages, codes, theories, ideologies, and methodologies for others to learn about and understand" (Schaafsma & Vinz, 2007, p.278). The process of narrative-telling, itself, "becomes a way of understanding exact experiences that are being scrutinized as stories of gathering places for meaning" (Gordon et al. 2007, p. 326). These stories convey the contexts, complexities, and "situatedness" of those exact experiences at that point in time (Gordon et al. 2007, p. 326). Schools, then, should not be viewed as a short-term culture that is situated as one snapshot in time. They are forever and constantly changing, just as the educators who teach and lead within those cultures are also constantly changing. Attitudes are also situational, not static, and for talent searches to delve deeper into candidates' emotions and beliefs, narrative snapshots that deal with real issues and complex topics can tell us more than traditional interview questions, résumés, or transcripts.

Carr (1986) reminds us that what is essential to a storyteller's position is the "advantage of real hindsight, a real freedom from the constraint of the present to occupy a position after, above, and outside of events simply narrated" (p. 60). Narratives offer such glimpses into the connectedness of the past, present, and futures of the storytellers (school staff members) who have past, present, and future beliefs and perceptions about working in schools and school districts, educational policies, procedures, and ethics.

According to Schaafsma & Pagnucci et al. (2007), composing stories reveals not only the people, places, and things we observe but also why we observe them and the significance that we invest in our own (human) observations (pp. 282–283). Narratives, like other good research, "allow us to hold up a mirror, see a reflection, turn it ever so slightly so we see a new angle, a new perception, or something beyond what we could see before the narration" (Schaafsma & Pagnucci et al., 2007, p. 284). The narrative, then, "illuminates and alters our perceptions and fills it in with the story, the ideologies, the methods, and the theories it reveals through the slants and positions" (Schaafsma & Pagnucci et al., 2007, p. 284). In short, this book promotes narratives as a stimulus for reflection and for understanding various "angles and perceptions" about those we wish to hire or do not wish to hire. We are looking for the best, remember.

The form that stories take in research holds a prominently high value as narratives appeal to humans due to their "every day, vernacular language" (Schaafsma & Vinz, 2007, p. 277). This enables virtually any reader to read constructed narratives and gain some understanding of why particular stories are being told. The use of ordinary language by narrative researchers is a deliberate ideological move, an attempt to make research more inclusive for readers (Schaafsma & Vinz, 2007, p. 277) and more authentic for all who engage in narrative theory processes. Narrative theory, then, holds high value among both quantitative and qualitative researchers. Gaining insights into the "stories behind the numbers" provides useful refractions for statistical results to capture human perspectives (Schaafsma & Vinz, 2007, p. 277). While this book does not use any quantitative methods,

Why Narratives?

it prescribes practical methods that can complement hiring practices across the globe. Narrative theory is its own science as story plotlines can build a significant glimpse into others' attitudes and dispositions in the educational workplace or any workplace environment.

Such qualitative insights (intricately "packed" into human stories), according to Goodall (2000), can bring about a better understanding of the role of narratives as a form of research, which can then be ultimately coined as the "new ethnographies" of qualitative research (p. 190). Narrative theory offers "an emerging alternative style of qualitative writing" (Perl et al., 2007, p. 309) that is based on the organizing principle for understanding human interactions (Riessman, 1993, p. 1) and attitudes about the identities embedded within those same stories. That book will illustrate this point later on.

The word "story" can be quite metaphoric and it is meant to demystify any kind of inhuman or impersonal research in education "as it draws attention to who was and wasn't allowed to speak with authority in a particular field" (Schaafsma & Pagnucci et al., 2007, p. 285). A simple goal of narrative research is "to weave narratives into the research and research into the narratives" (Perl et al., 2007, p. 324). What "counts" is who gets to tell the story, and so many varied audiences await learning from our own storytelling and responses to human narrative.

Narrative Theory and Practical Uses

As discussed earlier, this book uses "narrative" as a synonym for "story" in its simplest and most distilled meaning (Bell, 1988, p. 101). Before sharing the process of using narratives in human resources best practices for hiring educators, it is important to understand that the story is an account through which experiences are related in response to presented story lines. Narrative is the way of recounting, constituting, representing, and constructing the story. Using story and narrative as research is a situated activity that locates educators in a particular place and time—chiefly as narrator of those events (Bell, 1988, p. 101). Therefore, as educators tell their stories or respond to others' stories, they disable them within a certain context or point in time as they remember how a story took place (Bell, 1988, p. 101) or how an experience unfolded—which is highly emotional and full of mental response. These contexts open up avenues for narrativized life events that construct our attitudes and dispositions about a subject or topic that holds meaning for us. Where there is meaning and emotion, there is authenticity and truth. Hiring teams want to know the truth about the attitudes behind the person.

Rather than looking strictly at narrative structures, as outlined by Labov's (1972) structural approach—which include six categories of examining the narrative structure (abstract, orientation, complicating action, evaluation, resolution, and coda), this book will not examine the intricate discourse patterns or formal structures of such oral or written narratives. That is not the purpose or intention of this book, but it could better be explored in other future critical discourse books that deal with hiring or recruitment tactics within common places or themes, thus creating a discourse in education.

Instead, this book examines the potential and power of narrative theory for (re-) considering human resources practices as they are situated today in most school districts and organizations.

Narratives That Build Meaning From Exchanges With the "Other"

Though Perl et al. (2007) assert that we need to apply a new kind of criteria for analyzing narratives, those which take the readers' experiences into account and focus on language as a driving force for communicating our stories is the more important factor behind storytelling:

> Good stories strive to use relational language and narrative styles to create a purposeful dialogue between readers and the author. This dialogue proceeds through close, personal identification—and recognition of difference—of the reader's experiences, thoughts, and emotions, with those of the author. A good story is a good read. It gives pleasure, enlivens the imagination, and delights the senses. It appeals as a form of literature as well as a way of knowing. It teaches through its manner of expression as well as through its claims about the world.
>
> (Perl et al., 2007, pp. 307–308)

Understanding of the "self" in relation to the "other" moves our attention towards two major distinctions of the role that narrative plays in the presence of someone who: 1.) tells a story; 2.) responds to a story; and 3.) reflects on a story. What benefits individual interview committee members also benefits the entire team, both as a professional learning community and as individuals who desire to hear others' attitudes about similar situations so that attitude analysis becomes a new way of thinking about the craft of teaching, leading, and learning.

According to Witherell & Noddings (1991), two major ideas characterize the relationship between the "self" and the "other." First, the ways in which we define or are defined have to do with social and cultural contexts. Secondly, our relations with other persons have meaning systems which evolve from our mutual predicaments and possibilities (p. 85). Narratives, then, "assist us to give structure to our daily lives in the ways that we learn, what we perceive, what we value, and how we relate to each other" (pp. 85–86). Stories have the power to assist the interviewer to understand the "human responses" of the interviewee.

Narratives Build Socialized Intertextuality and Identity Shifting

Text, itself, merges the teller and the reader according to Bakhtinian perspectives that assist Bruner's (1990) insights regarding the narrative experience: "Texts do not appear in isolation, but in relation to other's texts" (Ball & Freedman, 2004, p. 53). Thus, our "speaking, reading, and writing, are in dialogue with each other constantly" (Ball & Freedman, 2004, p. 53). Narrative text ultimately provides us with opportunities to respond to text with our own text (or story).

Language and literature assist us to create spaces for ourselves as "individual actors within them" (Hall et al., 2005, p. 3) and are contextually based regarding our search for our own perceived reality. Text, or literature, then, is not the "other," but an exchange of the internal/external dialogic process that Bakhtinian theory stresses. It is important to understand that the "next [written] moment must not be a derivative of the previous moment." Context and exchanges forecast social activity and thought because "thinking [and writing] is experience based"

(Dewey, 1916, p. 153). Writing is thinking and thinking is writing. In this book, you will find stories that interviewees can respond to in order to understand their own attitudes about a specific topic or issue that is aligned with their organization's beliefs about students, learning, achievement, and the culture that surrounds them (the four SLAC creeds).

Narrative spaces become an inter-textual ground for contesting others' voices, re-accentuating their utterances with new meaning and "reinterpreting the self through another." Narratives become the actual zones for agentive possibilities, according to Wortham (2001):

> We carry out our written speech acts on the unfolding landscape of unfolding inter-texts and emergent structures of texts that ultimately condition our situation for future [professional] actions as constantly changing identity patterns that fluctuate even when reading across such textual boundaries. (p. 9)

Stories used for interviewing practices can embed powerful meaning strands that not only provide a platform for responding to stories, but they also act as a teaching tool that might assist educator-candidates to re-think a specific position about a topic or issue and thereby undergo identity-in-the-making. Your candidates will be learning something more about themselves while they are being interviewed by you and may decide to alter their identity beliefs about a topic after being exposed to new narrative situations.

Narratives provide a landscape and canvas for moving meaning-making into other spheres of new meaning. Therefore, we actually respond to others and write ourselves into new identities, socially and constantly, each and every minute, as such within an interview setting where narratives regenerate responsiveness to others' and our own emotions about a particular topic. Texts ultimately make their meaning in a world of surrounding texts, according to the highly relevant Bakhtinian theory (Ball & Freedman, 2004).

It is my aim that the creators of educational narratives will bring about greater social understandings about the identities of their candidates and the narratives themselves, and that this will ultimately provide an inter-textual study of school districts' hiring practices and candidates' attitudes, all working together at the same time.

Narratives and the Identity Behind Our Displayed Attitudes

While the narrative approach is well suited for studies of subjectivity and identity (Riessman, 1993, p. 5), narratives also provide deep insights into moral issues and, like all other social actors, educators might seek to convince others that they are good people (and good teachers, for that matter). As described above, interacting with narratives can inevitably be a self-reflection process (Riessman, 1993, p. 11). That will allow hiring committees to acquire such insights about candidates' attitudes and dispositions regarding highly controversial topics as they relate to our deep, foundational belief systems.

Narrators create plots from "disordered experience and give reality a unity that neither nature nor the past possesses so clearly" (Riessman, 1993, p. 4). Narratives embody ways for others to enter in to a conscious reflection and refraction of ideas mirroring that which might be experienced by someone else's own lived experiences. These "ways in" offer individuals social space by which they explore other galaxies of (professional) lives through the lens of human science research:

> Story presents the search in (re)search. The search manifests as the continuous playing out of lives and experiences. The (re) in story takes many forms—backward glances at the past and sideways glances at present contingencies. Stories move, and when they do, they have a way of informing and (re)searching the unfolding narrative as well as revealing and construing their authors and readers. These treks through the world focus on observation, worldview, feelings, questions, and temporary understandings. Stories celebrate these subjectivities in all their accompanying complexities.
> (Schaafsma & Vinz, 2007, p. 277)

Schaafsma & Vinz (2007) present thoughtful articulations about narratives having the power to "open profound spaces for learning, which are fertile and realizable" (p. 280). Through intimate dialogue and in communion (more than one conversation) with other beings, "one can learn to see differently and that seeing differently can change our conceptions of the world" (p. 281). By exchanging the narrative responses of school leaders, changing conceptions are natural outcomes of such an exchange.

Perl et al.'s (2007) work also values the enriching power that narratives have on understanding the role of using critical analysis for examining experiences when "one can seize upon the commonalities of experiences and urge one another towards more critical narrations of their experiences because narratives are more searing and real" (pp. 318–319).

In fact, Gee (1999) believes that "narratives cannot be separated from the socio-cultural and socio-historical contexts from which they emerge"; instead, they are "deeply embedded in socio-cultural discourses that represent socially mediated views of experience" (Johnson & Golombek, 2002, p. 5). Stories are simply packed with ideology and this book examines educators' perceptions of the cultural ideology of the world of teaching and educating children, not to mention the politics behind education, the decision-making that must be healthy for our students, and the support network of positivism that contributes to maintaining a healthy workplace. For example, a hot topic inside and outside the classroom is the politicization of education and the role that high-stakes testing plays in the evaluation of teachers. The opt-out movement is one of the most enormous political movements in education since segregation in schools. Wouldn't you desire to gain insights into the dispositions of teachers about such an important historic event before they step into your classrooms?

Although stories create such humanistic outlets for examining other ways of "doing critical business," Schaafsma & Pagnucci et al. (2007) contend that narratives also confront deeper emotional issues that stories can only truly capture. Once educators enter into emotional critiques of or respond to others' viewpoints, their attitudes about any educational topic shine through when telling stories or strategically utilizing narratives:

> Stories might come out arguing, being unable to agree on whether it is light or dark for helping them distinguish day from night. Some slip away unnoticed, just out of focus, just out of reach. They might turn their backs on us. Or, gaze right at us, demanding that we make them substantial. They sometimes get lost in our words. We sometimes lose ourselves before the boundaries are fixed. The urge to tell stories is powerful, and they bring us to life by allowing us to see ourselves and others caught in the becoming that is life.
>
> (Schaafsma & Pagnucci et al., 2007, p. 301)

Narratives do not accept static ideas or outcomes designed to anchor our lives; they usually "attempt to keep possibilities open, to allow for multiple interpretations, even fictional ones" (Schaafsma & Pagnucci et al., 2007, p. 301). Our attitudes about life represent our life and our beliefs. Talent searches need to extract candidates' attitudes.

Noddings (1984) describes stories as emotional catalysts for inquiry because "narratives embody deep emotions, such as frustration, fear, anger, and joy, and then they focus on caring emotions and actions of trust, dialogue, feelings, and responding" (p. 13). Hence, these emotional feelings can be confronted on moral planes whereby as theory and practice merge with one another, new identities can unfold and be re-told. Stories will elicit deep emotional responses that also reflect our moral standards.

Narratives Describe Position, Agency, and Truth

Situation and context also plays a role in framing one's perceptions, according to Bruner (1990): "What one thinks one did in a particular setting" plays a role in the reasons why a person might feel or act in a particular way (p. 119). Narratives are to be placed in a contextual framework of how a situation holds itself to be "true" to the actor in time, meaning, culture, and even within culturally normative functions. School environments contain all of these possibilities for exploring the agency of educators within their own perceptions about how they operate and function within a particular classroom setting or school culture, at large.

According to Kenyon & Randall (1997), "narratives pull out contextualized differences between public (professional) narratives and private (personal) narratives" (p. 49) while "surface storytelling" and "deep storytelling" might have blurry boundaries as professionals who wish to speak about a work situation with private feelings will become engaged to do so within social situations, such as an interview session.

Crites' (1971) work with teachers' narratives reveals the dialects of public versus private storytelling when notions about "the concepts of secret, sacred, and cover stories can encourage us to examine the stories that we tell; there are stories that are told that make us look good in the eyes of others" (Christiansen & Ramadevi, 2002, p. 101). At what point do educators reveal their own truths about a specific topic? Narratives often compel us to tell the truth because they evoke such emotion and the talent searches that are conducted in the educational arena need to understand the power of carrying out emotionally responsive topics for us to fully examine epistemologies or paradigms that educational professionals might possess.

Stories are told for certain reasons as feelings and such feelings "lie behind the stories that are told," according to Witherell & Noddings (1991): "Stories directly identify with what is moored in what the self has done, would do, or should ideally choose" (p. 124). Stories might capture what can be observed, but also what underpins the feelings behind an event that is narrated. This is the essence of going beyond résumés and transcripts.

Most importantly and highly relevant to this book is the role that narratives play in "talking back" to a systemic and, perhaps, more global discourse or problem that might be inherent within a school system. Czarniawska (1997) examined the role of narrativizing metaphor usage for the changing contexts of organizational worlds. Here, in Czarniawska's study of office workers, fact, and fiction were merged through the introduction to narrative theory models as organizational discourses which impacted those who worked within such systems of rigid office practices: "A scene was set, a problem introduced, characters described, tensions introduced to create an unfolding plot, and then there was some sort of climax and resolution" (Clandinin & Connelley, 2000, pp. 10–11). It appears that various types of rigid culture systems exist not only in the educational field, but in other business models, as well. When a problem is posed through narratives, we are compelled, as human beings, to respond to what we feel is the truth.

Geertz (1988) illustrates the importance of looking at how narratives provide insights into how the storyteller might be positioned within the larger operational context or structure of the world when he introduces the concept of "tentativeness" to narrative researchers:

> Tentativeness relates to the way in which one is positioned in the "parade." We know what we know because of how we are positioned. If we shift our position in the "parade," our knowing shifts. However, as the "parade" might also shift, our relative positions change. What we knew at one point in time shifts as the "parade" moves temporally forward to another point in time.
>
> (Clandinin & Connelley, 2000, p. 17)

Here, as actors on a stage or clowns in a "parade," educators' positions, identities, and larger social systems are attitude provoking. Yet, narrative research assists us in unraveling such complex systems for further understandings and the more we reveal about each other's understandings and attitudes about education, the better hire we will ultimately make because educators are also actors on the stages of professional and personal worlds and using narratives as a prompt and lens for understanding the human behind the story. This book unleashes a progressive field of proven research that goes beyond simply identifying the knowledge, skills, and abilities of school staff members in the educational workplace who hold particular feelings and emotions that we have never touched before when meeting someone new during an interview.

Profoundly introduced and relative to the issues raised above, Ritchie & Wilson's (2000) work with teacher narratives opens up powerful discourses about how teachers need to "reclaim and revise personal and professional identities so that they move from silent outsider [as a student] to authoritative insider [as a teacher]" (pp. 74–75). Here, teachers' narratives about their past experiences as students provide insights into how they were trained to be "good, abiding students" even though they now seek more open and productive relationships with their own students. They strive to operate in a system of education that has historically taught them differently in the past. Those who wish to reveal the greater social justice of education can ultimately lead to classrooms, better schools, and better school districts in the end, especially if those who sit before us have impeccable attitudes about complex, changing issues.

Work in the field of teacher constructed narratives illustrates the power of narrative to reveal and promote agency. For example, in Ritchie & Wilson's (2000) narrative-based study, one teacher, named Carol, exhibits a strong sense of agency through narrative documentations that elicit the power of "resisting, renaming, revising, and breaking out of being silenced" as she shares her stories about evolving into a constantly changing teaching professional:

> The past 12 years have transformed me. I've changed from being a person who let others dictate what I think and how I act to someone who is critically aware of the choices and possibilities in my life. I no longer regard events in life as "given," blindly

accepting what others say. I know that thoughts and actions are socially constructed, controlled by dominant ideologies and discourses. For a good portion of my life, I failed to question why things are the way that they are. I've learned to ask questions.
(Ritchie & Wilson, 2000, p. 91)

In this example, the power of narrative empowers the teller and Carol offers important snapshots into thoughts, ideas, and even past illusions about educational systems. The professional-in-action can exert an agency that constantly evolves and reflects. We cannot learn these types of human structures through examining paper résumés, cover letters, or by using generic interview questions.

Highlighting Carol's expressed desire to re-think her teaching life against constrained patterns of the system that she experienced as a student and trained as a teacher in, Davies (2005) defines agency as "the ability to recognize the constitutive power of discourse, the ability to catch discourse, structure, and practice in the act of shaping desire, perception, and knowledge, and the engagement in a collective process of re-naming, re-writing, and re-positioning oneself in relation to coercive structures" (p. 201).

Educators sometimes live in the "coercive structure" of a system that they create because we consistently hire teachers without ever matching the organization's desired attitudes against the attitudes that we look for in a candidate. While positioning deals with power and power can dominate our relationships, this book does not examine the topic of power. Instead, this book offers new ways to elicit a match between a school culture and the candidates that they hire who will ultimately be the best hires.

Holland et al. (1998) further provides a telling description of agency within our understanding of figurative identities—which uses narrativized story and dramaticized elements to extract lived events of human action: "Agency is improvisation—which is a significant form of renovation—and self-directed symbolization is also attributed to developing our picture of identity" (p. 277). Narratives expose our place within a system, our beliefs about rigid policies, and provide an outcome that assumes a greater responsibility for knowing more about the $2 million dollar hire that we make. If hiring quality educators is the most important factor that contributes to student learning and achievement, then why have we waited so long to find out exactly what our new hires really feel and believe about children, developmental capabilities, policy, or practices in education? This book will elevate your hiring selections to new heights.

Who Cares About Educators' Stories?

We do. Very little research exists regarding the role of narrative theory "counting as research" for hiring educators. Clandinin (2006) makes a remarkable link between the power of recognizing students' stories and shaping an administrator's stories to live by. Here, the idea of creating a school landscape through the recognition of others' stories is something that educators can reflect on in truly meaningful ways:

> Considering the narrative histories of school participants, which include their cultural histories, possibilities to scaffold between stories for building a wider story to live by could take a long time. Relationships take time to build. School landscapes shape more or less educative possibilities for building relational places out of which new stories mindful of families, children, teachers, and principals can be negotiated and lived out.
>
> (Clandinin, 2006, p. 111)

Within an educator's "figured world," (Holland et al., 1998) stories need to be told. For example, one might remember stories told by teachers in the copy-room which focus on some strange interactions with student and parents. I have heard many retiring teachers tell me that they are going to write a book about their life experiences within a school. Even administrators have stories to tell and there is some research in the field about using narrative theory to wrestle with the human business of being a school principal.

The work of Craig (2007) further supports the desire within qualitative research to investigate principals' perceptions through narrative inquiry for understanding leadership styles and struggles within accountability cultures. Speaking through metaphors of "dragons," Craig (2007) uncovered the feelings, beliefs, and perceptions of one high-school principal who leads within accountability and testing stressors and defines these "institutionalized dragons" as highways that are to be navigated by school leaders. In this case, the school leader resigned as a high-school principal because the stressors and power behind the educational accountability culture would not permit any comprehensive curriculum reform; instead, it demanded conformity to the accountability culture. Demands from his superiors focused on looking for "spiked test scores that revolved around the cultural desires for testing outcomes" and to define what "good schools" should be like (p. 1254).

Craig's (2004) earlier research in narrative theory used "story constellations" to bridge clusters of stories from different tellers within various schools across lines that would intersect and make sense of "potential interstices that developed through such story clusters" about distributed leadership practices (p. 163). Through her research, the interstices included gathering perceptions from school leaders that highlighted the backgrounds of school leaders that impacted their contextualized practices for years, despite the realities of school-leader turnover—which then ultimately led to the continuance of teacher-owned school reform (p. 189).

Connelly & Clandinin (1988) remind us that "as teachers listen, read, write, and discuss professional narratives, they articulate their personal philosophies, explore their values, and evaluate their decisions, not in a detached way, but out of the experience of their own practices" (p. 33). Instead, narratives offer "images about how teachers use their past experiences in instructional situations," (Clandinin, 1986, p. 8), and other educators can do the same.

The modality of social construction through narrative-knowing acknowledges educators as "craft-artists" within the profession that they construct and author each day (Blumberg, 1989; Mack, 2007). Writing about themes through which educators might find "victorious" or even those with which they might "struggle" with each day, school leaders can reflect on their current realities as they strive to gain mastery of knowing themselves as situated "actors" on the stage of being an educator within trying times, budget crises, or anti-public school educational platforms within governmental discourse.

The work in this book was originally inspired by principals' perceptions of high-stakes testing as it relates to leadership functions within a culture of increased accountability. Through principals' "told" stories, identities were examined through politicized educational initiatives that had become blurred for them. This was explored in my 2010 dissertation *Examining School Leaders' Narratives as a Lens for Understanding Leadership Identity and Agency Within a High-Stakes Testing Culture of Accountability*.

Hiring Practices and Narrative Theory

It is so important to bring narrative theory into hiring practices and talent search processes. It is a highly successful practice at the Elm Grove and Gardenville school districts which we will discuss later in Chapters 5 and 6. I've seen it work in the districts where I have worked during my 17-year career in education. You will have better insights into the candidates that you meet. Narrative tools will assist you in finding the best hire.

Kersten's (2008) research of Illinois principals' perceptions of hiring practices reveals that principals have a dominant responsibility for hiring school staff and the traits that make them feel more comfortable about a candidate are interviewees who display friendly, caring, tactful, humorous, and empathetic attitudes (p. 364). Yet, this study did not utilize narrative theory constructs; it simply surveyed school leaders about their perceptions of what they desire in a "good hire."

Metzger and Wu (2008) look at commercialized teacher hiring instruments, i.e. Gallup's Teacher Perceiver Interview (TPI) instrument, and analyze the link between using such an instrument in teacher hiring—in order to mine for affective beliefs, attitudes, and values (p. 921) within their candidate pools. They find a modest link through their synthesis of 24 studies, but many of the studies had complications with their scales and surveys. Again, narrative tools were not used.

Ralph, Kesten, and Lang (1998) discovered through surveying 70 directors of education in Canada the qualities most desired in new teachers were: 1. strong interpersonal communication and 2. effective in classroom management/discipline skills (p. 47). While these were categorical desires, nowhere were attitudes uncovered through their recruitment and hiring processes.

Within this supplemental on-line chapter, I cite many references that have built the foundation for narrative theory and narrative inquiry for centuries.

Certainly, there have been books written since the 1990s and early 2000s about storytelling and narrative theory, and there are books hitting the market regarding storytelling and leadership, storytelling and motivation, and the power of storytelling. Below, you will find two modern books that describe useful techniques for your hiring practices:

- *162 Keys to School Success*, by Franklin Schargel
- *The Principal as Human Resources Leader*, by M. Scott Norton

As you think about the big picture of your own talent searches, reserve a spot for narrative theory. By the end of this book, you will have read about success stories in the field of education where narratives were used to mine for attitudes and dispositions within human resource responsibilities. Most likely, you will have identified with the issues that are presented through narrative construction. Let's begin to roll out the process of how to begin a journey of powerful hiring practices at your school as we move ahead to Chapter 4.

References

Altman, R. (2008). *A theory of narrative*. New York: Columbia University Press.
Ball, A.F., & Freedman, S.W. (Eds.) (2004). *Bakhtinian Perspectives on Language, Literacy, and Learning*. Cambridge: Cambridge University Press.
Bell, S. E. (1988). Becoming a political woman: The reconstruction and interpretation of experience through stories. In A. D. Todd & S. Fisher (Eds.), *Gender and discourse: The power of talk* (pp. 97–123). Norwood, NJ: Ablex.
Blumberg, A. (1989). *School administration as a craft: Foundations of practice*. Boston, MA: Allyn and Bacon.
Bruner, J. (1990). *Acts of meaning*. Cambridge, MA: Harvard University Press.
Bruner, J. (1986). *Actual minds, possible worlds*. Cambridge, MA: Harvard University Press.
Carr, D. (1986). *Time, narrative, and history*. Bloomington: Indiana University Press.
Christiansen, H., & Ramadevi, S. (2002). *Reeducating the educator: Global perspectives on community building*. New York: State University of New York Press.
Clandinin, D. J. (1986). *Classroom practice: Teacher images in action*. London: The Falmer Press.
Clandinin, D. J. (2006). *Composing diverse identities: Narrative inquiries into the interwoven lives of children and teachers*. New York: Routledge.
Clandinin, D. J., & Connelly, M. F. (2000). *Narrative inquiry: Experience and story in qualitative research*. San Francisco, CA: Jossey-Bass Publishers.

Collins, J. (2001). *Good to great: Why some companies make the leap and other's don't*. New York: Harper Business.

Connelly, F. M., & Clandinin, D. J. (1988). *Teachers as curriculum planners: Narratives of experience*. New York: Teachers College Press.

Craig, C. J. (2004). The dragon in school backyards: The influence of mandated testing on school contexts and educators' narrative knowing. *Teachers College Record, 106 (6)*, 1229–1257.

Craig, C. J. (2007). Narrative Inquiries of Geographically Close Schools: Stories given, lived, and told. *Teachers College Record, 109 (1)*, 160–191.

Crites, S. (1971). The narrative quality of experience. *Journal of American Academy of Religion, 39 (3)*, 291–311.

Czarniawska, B. (1997). *Narrating the organization: Dramas of institutional identity*. Chicago, IL: University of Chicago Press.

Davies, B. (2005). *Shards of glass*. Cresskill, NJ: Hampton Press.

Dewey, J. (1916). *Democracy and education: An introduction to the philosophy of education*. New York: Macmillan.

Gee, J. P. (1999). *An introduction to discourse analysis*. New York: Routledge.

Geertz, C. (1988). *Works and Lives: The anthropologist as author*. Stanford, CA: Stanford Press.

Goodall, H.L. (2000). *Writing the new ethnography*. New York: Rowman & Littlefield.

Gordon, E., McKibbin, K., Vasudevan, L., & Vinz, R. (2007). Writing out of the unexpected: Narrative inquiry and the weight of small moments. *English Education, 39 (3)*, 326–351.

Hall, J.K., Vitanova, G., & Marchenkova, L. (Eds.) (2005). *Dialogue with Bakhtin on second and foreign language learning*. Mahwah, NJ: Lawrence Erlbaum Associates.

Holland, D., Lachicotte Jr., W., Skinner, D., & Cain, C. (1998). *Identity and agency in cultural worlds*. Cambridge, MA: Harvard University Press.

Jetter, R. (2010). *Examining school leaders' narratives as a lens for understanding leadership identity and agency within a high-stakes testing culture of accountability*. Dissertation, State University of New York at Buffalo.

Johnson, K. E., & Golombek, P. R. (2002). *Teachers' narrative inquiry as professional development*. Cambridge, UK: Cambridge University Press.

Kenyon, G. M., & Randall, W. L. (1997). *Restorying our lives: Personal growth through autobiographical reflection*. Westport: Praeger.

Kersten, T. (2008). Teacher hiring practices: Illinois principals' perspectives. *The Educational Forum, 72 (4)*, 355–368.

Labov, W. (Ed.) (1972). The transformation of experience in narrative syntax. In W. Labov (Ed.), *Language in the inner city: Studies in the Black English vernacular* (pp. 354–396). Philadelphia: University of Pennsylvania Press.

Mack, B. W. (2007). Learning the principalcraft: Experiencing and reflecting. *School Administrators Association of New York State Journal, 1 (36)*, 13–15.

Metzger, S., & Wu, M-J. (2008). Commercial teacher selection instruments: The validity of selecting teachers through beliefs, attitudes, and values. *Review of Educational Research, 78 (4)*, 921–940.

Noddings, C. (1984). *Caring: A feminine approach to ethics and moral education*. Berkeley: University of California Press.

Norton, S. (2014). *The principal as human resources leader: A guide to exemplary practices for personnel administration*. New York: Routledge.

Perl, S., Counihan, B., McCormack, T., & Schnee, E. (2007). Storytelling as scholarship: A writerly approach to research. *English Education, 39 (3)*, 306–325.

Polkinghorne, D. E. (1988). *Narrative knowing and the human sciences*. New York: State University of New York Press.

Ralph, E., Kesten, C., & Lang, H. (1998). Hiring new teachers: What do school districts look for? *Journal of Teacher Education, 49 (1)*, 47–56.

Riessman, C. K. (1993). *Narrative analysis*. London: Sage.

Ritchie, J. S., & Wilson, D. (2000). *Teacher narrative as critical inquiry: Rewriting the script*. New York: Teachers College Press.

Schaafsma, D., Pagnucci, G. S., Wallace, R. M., & Stock, P. L. (2007). Composing storied ground: 4 generations of narrative inquiry. *English Education, 39 (3)*, 282–305.

Schaafsma, D., & Vinz, R. (2007). Composing narratives for inquiry. *English Education, 39 (4)*, 277–281.

Schargel, F. (2010). *162 keys to school success: Be the best, hire the best, train, inspire, and retain the best*. New York: Routledge.

Witherell, C., & Noddings, N. (1991). *Stories lives tell: Narrative and dialogue in education*. New York: Teachers College Press.

Wortham, S. (2001). *Narratives in action: A strategy for research and analysis*. New York: Teachers College Press.

Zinsser, W. (1987). *Inventing the truth: The art and craft of memoir*. Boston, MA: Houghton Mifflin Company.

Getting Your Resources and Team Ready

Officer . . . I saw this kid come barreling down the street . . . as if he had no sense of direction . . . no regard for anything or anyone else around him . . . and I watched him drive his car into the parade float . . . like he hated that float or something. I don't know what happened. It was a split second. A split second! I blinked and it was all over. I don't know why he would do something like that. I'm glad that he is OK, but the float . . . oh my GOD, what a mess! I cannot believe that this float is ruined. The student council worked so hard on it. It was the best one this school ever saw. That float represented Trenton High School's alma mater and soul!

(Mr. Tyler, Assistant Principal)

If you were a police officer, your goals and reasons for becoming a police officer would be different from those if you were a teacher; each school district in the world is different from the one down the street and each school within that respective district is unlike the next. Charter schools and private schools are all different, as well. Sure, students fill the school, teachers check their mailboxes when they arrive in the morning, but each school has a different culture, unique demographics, and unique circumstances regarding their geographic location, surrounding community, and so much more.

Mr. Tyler works in a rural school district where parade floats are viewed as "gold." To destruct a parade float is "the straw that broke the camel's back" in Mr. Tyler's school district. Mr. Tyler places an importance on something other than the student who could have been injured as represented within this narrative. He states that he was glad that the student was OK, but then spends too much time bereaving his school's float. The balance between focusing on the possibly injured student but respecting the school district's culture and sense of pride is in conflict. Fall and spring parades at Trenton High School make their district a place of celebration. Here, culture is important, but not as important as the student's life.

What is sometimes different among staff candidates is the perception of the kind of staff members that we desire to hire versus those we do hire to work with and teach in our schools. One of my previous principals told me that he liked to hire English Language Arts (ELA) teachers for any position that called for an open certification to fulfill a position, such as a suspension room teacher, attendance counselor, or a study skills teacher.

But, what if this principal cannot find a quality ELA teacher? Does he look elsewhere? What are his criteria for hiring such a person to fill those jobs? Would a principal then try to look for someone who was male or female without revealing to anyone his real desires about which gender would best fit the school culture at that moment of hire?

The point is we all have inclinations about whom we would ideally like to hire, even if it isn't scientific at all. We are all human and we all have likes, dislikes, and pre-judgments about everything. Although we should not discriminate against others' viewpoints as compared to our own, we struggle to make the right decisions because we all have our own pre-dispositions and attitudes. What is especially important within this example is that narrative theory will force fairness within process for gathering candidates and selecting a finalist.

This chapter focuses on preparing you to implement your hiring process by getting everything that you need in order before you enact the implementation phase for your talent searches.

Selecting the Narrative Style and Tool

Narratives, as explored in Chapter 3, can bend identity exploration in a number of ways depending on how the tools are used. Rather than only thinking about crafting narratives that others must respond to, you can also have candidates write a story about a selected topic that will help you to know more about how they feel and act.

You can start an interview simply by asking candidates to "write a story of no less than 150 words about a time when you were a child and experienced a mean teacher or adult." You will be amazed with the results you get. You can attach further directions for their writing, such as "Describe what you learned from this experience," or "What would you like the committee to remember about your experience?" You will receive deeply rooted emotional responses with a story or lesson learned attached at the end, and these types of narratives or stories will go a long way in building a collective, reflective process within your organization.

In the upcoming chapters, you will see how the Elm Grove Central School District also went so far as to create an environment where interview stories were used for staff development (of their current staff members) for reinforcing the core set of beliefs that their organization abides by and carries out.

You don't have to get so caught up with the specific narrative style or tools used. Instead, think about what you wish to learn about a candidate, what your organization's core beliefs are, and how you want to draw out or evoke emotional responses from your candidates to find out what they feel about the scenarios that you paint.

Selecting the Narrative Writer

Almost anyone can create the actual narratives that will be used for interview processes, because as Chapter 3 outlined, everyone has a story to tell. When hiring a math teacher for your school, your committee might consist of: the principal, a few teachers, support staff, maybe even the head custodian, and, perhaps, a parent or student. Each of these people has a different perception and angle on the position that you are hiring for in your school. This is a very good thing and it is fair to your students because they will benefit from the varied perspectives of the different professionals who lead their classrooms or school. But remember, the rationale behind narrative theory is to collect narrative data, to analyze it and use it to make better-informed decisions about a candidate.

You may want to select someone who is a creative writer. If you cannot select a creative writer within your committee, find someone who can do this within your school or district. If that is not doable, then ask an outside expert to craft narratives that build an inherent match to your agreed-upon committee criteria. Sometimes, it is very strategic to have the narrative-tool creator lead the brainstorming for a school on the four SLAC creeds, which will be outlined below. Anyone can write a story, and that is all that it should be. Just insert a few areas that press the emotions of your candidates so they have no choice but to respond or state something unique to a situation.

What this does, not only for your committee but also for your professional staff members who happen to be invited to your interview committee, is to provide professional development on the art of writing, reflecting, and motivating staff and students alike. At what point do your students understand the art of narrative theory and become able to negotiate through this creative avenue of art? I've even asked students to create narratives without telling them that it is for an interview. Look at what one of my previous students created when my committee was looking for narratives to explore the belief that teachers should care about all of the extremes of intellect that their students might display:

> *Gordon, one of my best friends, came to school with sneakers on and his hair slicked up in a Mohawk on exam day. His parents hated that Gordon watched YouTube for two to three hours a day. What they hated most about Gordon was that he hardly ever studied, but he got good grades on all of his tests. Gordon's parents begged Gordon's teachers to fail him because he never turned in any homework assignments and homework was a major responsibility that he should learn once and for all. Gordon's parents hated that Gordon had been getting away with doing nothing since he started high school and enough was enough for his parents.*
>
> *(Josh Sandberg, Grade 11)*

Here, Josh helped the Berry Park School District to create a narrative that would reveal the different perspectives on who should fail a grade versus who should be entitled to a grade promotion. What one student might study for three hours, a different student might not have to even review for one minute. The issue for Berry Park candidates to examine had to do with defining promotion requirements. Should Gordon not be allowed to move on to Grade 12?

I would suggest that whoever is creating the narratives to be used by a committee incorporates the following four key points. These will help your narratives to evoke the most emotion and have the greatest power in gleaning the attitudes that will help you to better differentiate between the candidates seated at your table:

1. The narrative must be a real example or sample of something that has happened, and it has to be something that is not far-fetched. It has to be believable and represent conversation as it would exist, naturally.

    Notice the differences between the two narratives below about a teacher who is obsessed with homework:

    I like to give my students homework every night. I like to see what they can and cannot do. I know that I don't grade every assignment, but that is fine with me. I know that they are going to do it because I threaten to grade it.

    It's like . . . giving my kiddos homework every darn night. Can they do it or blow it? Can they do it or lose it? Are their dogs eating their stuff or are sewer drains gobbling up their homework? I dunno. Those kids will lie to me, yep . . . and trust me . . . they will. But, I will threaten to grade every last one of their assignments. It teaches those little buggers responsibility!

    Conversational narratives evoke more emotion and are more likely to get to the heart of the reader or responder than narratives that are generic and bland. Remember, attitudes about issues must be drawn out as much as you can with your own writing power.

2. The narratives must reflect the established criteria in a number of ways so that the candidates can be differentiated based on their responses.
3. The rubrics being used to assess the narratives must be in alignment with one another (discussed more in Chapter 6).
4. Most importantly, the narratives must be agreed upon by the entire committee. Consensus in this case, must be unanimous.

Your interview team sets up the process from the start and the buy-in that takes place is easier than you think—especially if you follow the process outlined in this chapter. I have seen it unfold and be highly successful. The educational professionals of the Elm Grove and Gardenville school districts (outlined in Chapters 7 and 8) have seen the process unfold and they have become incredibly pleased with how stories get to the heart of what they really want to know about a candidate beyond the résumés and transcripts that were sitting somewhere on their desks.

Using the Four SLAC Creeds

As you can see from the sub-headings in this section, SLAC stands for students, learning, achievement, and culture. It is an acronym that will create purpose within your process and keep all that is important in mind from the start. Brainstorming in each of these areas should take place for each new position that is posted because each position requires different skills, though not necessarily different attitudes.

For instance, let's use the special education teacher example that was outlined earlier. A skill might be to have a candidate identify how to legally and appropriately restrain a student who is causing danger to him or herself, or others, when there is a student meltdown in the classroom. There is specialized training that would assist a teacher to do this appropriately and legally, obviously.

However, what if your committee believes that to represent your school appropriately, a staff member must first be an expert in identifying the potential for emotional unrest before it unfolds? What if your committee believes that the art of de-escalation tactics supersedes everything else that is embodied within the following example? Well, then you write your narrative in such a way that mines for that attitude:

> *I saw Chris crumple up his paper, throw it at the teacher, and head for Brooke with a pair of scissors. He was upset that she broke up with him through a note that was passed in class. He looked like he was going to stab her . . . oh my God . . . and it happened all in one second!*
>
> *(Jane, Grade 9 Classroom Aide)*

Here, a question about restraint or any other topic relative to this situation about emotional disabilities might appear to be about restraint, or it might be more about your committee's attitude about the untold story that led up to this situation in the first place. The more desired response might be about recognizing the piece of paper that was passed, or the relationship between Chris and Brooke, versus the quick end-result of having to restrain Chris who appeared to be going after Brooke with scissors. If a candidate answers nothing along the lines of recognizing any type of precursor before Chris became upset, then he or she does not have the correct attitudes relevant to this situation. If there is no care or understanding about what Chris might be feeling—another attitude that is desired by the committee to be displayed somewhere in the written response—then the candidate isn't suitable to be on your staff because the reponse does not align itself with how your committee feels about early warning signs, violence prevention, or kids with emotional disabilities, in general.

Each position within your school might have different scenarios or experiences that others might not have experienced. Maybe an outside maintenance worker will never experience anything like an alleged stabbing in class. Each position needs to be brainstormed for each category. That will give you your potential narrative tools to draw from as you search for the attitudes that will best fit your school in all staffing areas.

Students

Some brainstorming topics within the category of "students" might include (but are not limited to) unique topics that pose potential questions—based on the position being examined for hire. Remember, schools and school districts are obviously in business because of our students. Therefore, this category should look specifically at these types of categorical features for students: attendance, nutrition, school safety, discipline, bullying, relationships with other students, relationships with teachers, and relationships with administrators.

For a custodian, your committee's desired skills might be different from your principal's skills, but both should have the same attitudes about students since they both work in the same organization. The idea here is not to have robots work for you, but if the organization feels that there is a way to behave or perceive students then all personnel should align with that central goal. Look at the following narrative used to mine for interesting attitudes for hiring a head custodian:

> *My job is to keep this place clean. Period. If there are papers and trash on the floor, then they probably weren't important*

enough to even reach the trash can, so it is up to me to keep this place sparkling and clutter free. That is why I am here. I don't get involved with wondering why there is gum on the bottom of a table, why there are papers on the floor, or why there is spray painted graffiti on one of the bathroom walls. My job is to remove it or clean it.

(Earl, Retired Head Custodian)

While the skills (and now attitudes) of a custodian might be to "be aware of the garbage on the floor because it could assist the school with what is being thrown out by mistake," the attitude that should be inherent for both a custodian or principal is: "be aware of your surroundings" or "all can assist in the problem-solving of the organization even when it involves graffiti." Perhaps, it is the head custodian who notices certain students in certain places throughout the day? Maybe, the custodian knows the connotation behind some of the spray-painted initials that are part of the graffiti?

Sometimes, we ignore the attitudes behind everyone's position and the research presented in this book supports the importance of using narratives for uncovering the attitudes and dispositions of all staff—especially when we look carefully at the Elm Grove and Gardenville school districts in Chapters 5 and 6.

Impressive data regarding the reality about these two school districts and their new hires over the past two years demonstrates the usefulness and creativity behind the link between mining for attitudes using narrative theory models and the success of the candidates who were hired. These professionals can truly be called the best school staff members.

Each school district that is discussed in this book is able to report the following five successes about their new hires when narrative theory models were used:

1. There have been no disciplinary charges for any of their hires.
2. No resignations or transfers (either voluntary or involuntary) have occurred.
3. Parent or student complaints (about a staff member's judgment, behavior in the workplace, or on-the-job performance) have been almost non-existent.

4. Staff-to-staff relations have been impeccable.
5. Staff performance reviews have also been exceedingly positive and the staff members hired in the school districts illustrated in this book have reported that they are happy (both professionally and personally) in their positions.

It sounds too good to be true. But, the idea here is that narratives will assist you greatly as you mine for attitudes and dispositions in the workplace before a contract is offered.

Learning

After recognizing the importance of students in the organization and knowing that the reason for the existence of schools is for students to learn, your hiring committee might brainstorm some useful subtopics regarding learning. These might include instructional tactics to be used in the school, attitudes about best teaching practices, differentiation techniques for varied learning, student grouping ideals, management of the learning environment, gender implications in the classroom, and even recognizing the notion of the necessity of adult learning/training within the organization. Again, an approach to mining for attitudes in the workplace focuses on learning as the main objective in what the organization is supposed to do each day.

But, how might this look when hiring a cafeteria monitor? Maybe the narrative tool to be used, as decided by the interview committee, includes an idea about homework:

> *I tell these kids all the time . . . the cafeteria is a place for eating, not doing your homework. They should have done their 'homework' at 'home' like the word 'homework' describes! Then, I have to come around, try to clean the tables so the next class can come in to eat, and all I get are kids telling me not to get their papers wet with my soapy rag. These kids will never learn . . . oh, what a headache they give me.*
>
> (Joanne, Cafeteria Monitor)

Here, this brief constructed narrative by the interview committee was written with the reverse desired response in mind: that it is OK to do homework in lunch. The committee's belief about homework is that sometimes kids do not have a home-life that supports the importance of homework, or that their students do not have a table and chair at their house in order to work on their homework at "home."

Maybe it just isn't "cool" to be seen going home from school with books in hand. The idea here is that no staff member is immune to issues about learning. Each and every role in the workplace deals with learning even if it doesn't appear so and we want all of our staff members to know how serious the organization is about focusing on learning.

Achievement

After learning comes achievement. This category might include ideas or themes about assessments, testing, data collection, expectations for achievement, school rankings, portfolios, and so much more. On one hand, hiring a school nurse might not seem like it has anything to do with student achievement, but on the other hand, it is incredibly important.

Look at what Nancy has to say about her job as she hopes that the candidates being interviewed agree with her perception about her place within a school:

> *I do not only provide epi-pens for kids who have an emergency or give medication to a child who has ADHD. I am here because we are all focused on student achievement together. I do what I do because keeping kids healthy is necessary for them to learn and achieve. This is not an office to be known only for its Band-Aids, but an office where we get kids 'patched up' so they can get back to class and learn. A lot of school nurses do not see this as part of their job. But, I recognize this as a HUGE part of my job.*
> (Nancy, Elementary School Registered Nurse)

Nancy's narrative was constructed to get an agreement response from the nurse candidates who went through a formal interview and to teach candidates that achievement is also part of a school nurse's job. Not only that, but a more desired response would be to recognize other school health and safety precautions that will keep kids in classrooms and ultimately help them to better achieve. If a nurse candidate does not demonstrate some sort of agreement with this narrative, they are no longer considered to be a "good" candidate in the process. However, agreeing with this narrative seems obvious. So, the interview team had a complementing question to go along with the narrative analysis. This question was, "In what ways can you get kids back to class as quickly as possible, but without risking the potential of a real health concern that needs students to stay out of class or be picked up by a parent to go home?" The undesirable/desirable responses could be answers that have to do with head lice, fevers past a certain degree point, dizziness, and so on.

Remember, narratives do not only mine for a response to a particular idea, but they also help others to reflect, refract, and bend meaning into new ways of learning as described in Chapter 2. Achievement for a nurse, for example, might be focused and aligned with the total organization of school nurse leaders, not just school nurse managers.

Culture

Each school culture has a unique set of norms, processes, practices, and even overall personality. You already know this. While we sometimes try to conceive standardized practices across our entire organization, we are often left with the reality that each school is different. That is OK. That is why I lobby for schools to build a narrative process from scratch, rather than just cutting and pasting each other's narrative tools that were used in the past. I have worked with interview committee teams and have trained dozens and dozens of committees to create a process that works for them. Nothing is cookie-cutter. While this book includes different samples of narratives that have been used in other organization's hiring processes, it is not a recommended practice to just borrow others' narratives. They are unique to each organization as each culture is unique.

For example, think about your own knowledge of your school's budget, uniqueness of facilities, level of community involvement, creation of policies, extra-curricular activities, events that are special to the community, cultural diversity and/or demographic relevance to your educational institution, location of external resources in your area, level of school pride, and so much more. These are often different for us, and even the culture of having a school mascot might be fun and funny for one school (an alligator or hawk), but more controversial for the next (Indian or red devil).

The school culture is one of the most enjoyable portions of the SLAC creeds for schools to talk about and I have witnessed some highly creative and highly unique narratives and interview questions over the past four years. Notice the set of attitudes that are being mined for with the unique narrative sample about culture that is authored by a school board president as outlined below:

> Here in Huntington, we enjoy holding events right after school hours or even in the morning in many cases. We have a lot of second shift working parents in our community who don't arrive home until 7:00 a.m., so holding an event right after 7:30 a.m. is something that we pride ourselves in doing for our community. On the one hand, there could be some issues with those who are free at 6:00 p.m.; on the other hand, the turn-out for our events will most likely increase and the public might come to our board of education meetings more frequently. We are not sure what to do at this point, but we know that we are interested in doing something.
> (Ron, Board of Education President)

This narrative was given to superintendent candidates of the Huntington School District. The desired response for the board of education members who created this narrative example was to somehow preserve the culture of their district and maintain a high level of respect for their traditions while understanding their next superintendent's potential problem-solving skills for recognizing parents' work schedules, and then to move forward with a plan of action for the board.

Deeper Interviewing

As described in this chapter, using narratives within your screening process is a great way to narrow down your candidate pool. Narratives can also be used in your actual formal interview process and final interview process. You might even choose to set aside 20 minutes before each scheduled interview to have candidates sit and think about one narrative that is incredibly important to your organization, or peruse smaller narrative scenarios that they will have to verbally respond to during the interview. Not all narrative tools need to demand written results, as long as you have a rating scale devised to use during your interview so that there is a tracking system to recall each candidate's answers and who fared the best.

However, I would always recommend acquiring a written response for your narratives since the process of writing takes on a higher level of cognitive response through the processing of information from the brain down to the pen or computer.

I have seen some creative uses of different types of writing tasks among school district interviewing tools, but these seldom attack the essence of finding out about a candidate's attitudes. These types of straight-forward basic writing tasks strive to learn more about a candidate's writing capability instead of taking the opportunity to extract some writing samples from a candidate and then analyze them more in terms of displayed attitudes and dispositions. Here are three typical writing tasks that I have seen some interview teams engage in.

1. The "write a letter to" example:

    You find out that one of your buses got into an accident. Write a letter to parents explaining the steps that you took to investigate this matter.

    The rationale behind writing letters about processes or steps to be taken during a school emergency-closing decision or some other event are often a dead-end writing task that do not touch upon the attitudes and dispositions of a candidate.

2. The "identify a problem" example:

    You find that your students are regularly skipping your third-period class. What will you do to get more information about why this is happening?

    Sometimes, these scenarios have the power to become narrative tools because they might be about real human issues, but the ways that they are designed (by using a third-person narration style) only make them summaries and not real-life testimonials.

3. The "read over this policy" example:

    Please read Policy 6030 which is about prohibiting alcohol and drugs on school grounds. What revisions would you make to this policy?

All of these typical writing tasks are meant purely to uncover a candidate's knowledge, skills, and abilities for identifying chief job-related responsibilities according to the position and processes that will be learned over time. They do not offer any attitude analysis, and such writing tasks only use rubrics that judge the writer's content and attention to systematic grammar, punctuation, legibility, and spelling.

Interview Questions That Mine for Attitudes

The intent of this book is to assist you with supplementing your regular interview process with narrative-based tools that search for the best future employee attitudes. However, you should take a moment to recognize the difference between creating generic interview questions (that seek to understand a candidate's knowledge, skills, and abilities) with semantic alternatives that will change the entire premise of an interview question. With some simple tweaking these questions will offer more attitude analysis opportunities.

Let's say that you are interviewing candidates for a new principalship at your school. Let's look at some typical interview questions and then some alternatives for constructing questions that mine for attitudes. Just by revising the questions with some semantic changes, you will ultimately shift your candidate's answers. This will enable you to have your committee re-think their original questions and whether they are seeking skill-based answers or attitudinal responses. See Table 4.1 in order to see some sample interview question conversions for attitude analysis.

Here, notice the difference in answers that you will most likely get just by playing around with the wording of your questions. Instead of asking candidates to state their answers or explain a process, ask them how they feel about something, or ask them to react to something. Blatantly ask them about their attitudes about a topic or to offer some advice about a topic. Ask them to think retrospectively and introspectively. Don't just settle for questions about their knowledge. You can create a balanced process for looking at a candidate's knowledge, skills, abilities, and attitudes. Together with narrative tools, constructing a total search for the best workplace attitudes can help to place a spotlight on the regular responsibilities of the job

Table 4.1

Skill-Based Interview Questions	Attitude-Based Alternatives
1. What process would you use for solving your school's low attendance rate?	1. Describe how you feel about attendance policies.
2. How would you go about establishing your vision for the school, and how would you get others to follow your vision?	2. React to the words "vision" or "mission statement."
3. Define the top three duties of an assistant principal.	3. Do you need an assistant Principal? Please explain why or why not.
4. What do you know about high-stakes assessments and student achievement?	4. What are your attitudes toward high-stakes tests? Tell us a story about student achievement.
5. Tell us about your experiences with teaching students or leading teachers when dealing with students' emotional disabilities.	5. Do you have any parenting advice for parents who have a child who is emotionally disabled? Offer some words of wisdom to the teachers who teach students with emotional disabilities.
6. What types of professional development activities have you engaged in this past year?	6. Tell us about something that excites you.
7. What makes you the best candidate for becoming the next principal of our school?	7. What types of attitudes did you wish your own high school principal had while you were growing up?

that demand a certain level of expertise. But, again, be sure to be able to measure your candidate's responses in a manner that is scientific, objective, and fair. Later, Chapter 4 will help you more with how to analyze your candidates' answers to your authored narratives.

Putting It All Together

Let's say you need to hire a music teacher and you need to meet with your committee before you look at the applicant pool. At this point, remember, you don't even know who the applicants are. As you come up with your established criteria and brainstorm the four SLAC creeds, you find that you are looking for the following (non-negotiable) characteristics in your new music teacher based on the culture and past experiences of your school. Let's say that four of these characteristics are:

1. A music teacher who plans lessons with classroom teachers (because you haven't always had such collegiality within your school).
2. A music teacher who uses musical theory about rhythm to assist reading progress (because research in the music field is uncovering great literacy advances in this area).
3. A music teacher who doesn't view himself or herself as just the school's music teacher (because your school district feels that identity is important when looking at professional success).
4. A music teacher who believes that students should view music as a life necessity, not a life additive (because philosophically, the school culture you work in believes this to be true).

As you craft your interview questions to include some of the types of generic questions outlined in this chapter, you start to design your narratives or questions to support these four major SLAC creed areas. One of the interview team members creates such narratives that test for these issues and then you finalize some narratives that draw out your thematic SLAC creeds, one of which might include this longer narrative tool:

> *I get the whole thing about collaboration and working with others so that the students have a better learning experience. That's all well and good, but the reality is that I have no time during a day to plan with five different grade level teachers, nor do I have any clue about how to teach reading or mathematics. So many classroom teachers think that their class is more important than music.*

> *They send kids late to my class, get upset if I send them late to their class and the principal also schedules music out, completely, if there is a half-day or special event. Yeah . . . I know some basics of how to infuse some learning points with social studies, but I am a music teacher . . . through and through . . . and it is my job to teach music appreciation and style. That is what the students deserve to get out of music class. That is what the love and appreciation of music includes and that is why I was hired by this district.*
>
> *(Grace Edwards, Music Teacher)*

Just this one narrative offers so many points that you might wish to examine in all of your candidates. There are "correct" responses to this narrative and there are "incorrect" responses, according to your desired responses. What each candidate extracts to be important or unimportant is based on the opportunity that you are giving them to demonstrate to you that they are the best candidate for the job. Again, it is important to be very specific about the SLAC creeds that you decide to exploit and the narrative examples that you use for candidates to respond to or to create themselves.

As you meet some really great candidates who were recruited, screened, and who are now sitting in front of you at the interview stage, you then look at what you have examined so far: résumés, transcripts, cover letters, and reference letters. You have lots of paper or computer files. You decide to go further. You take a little time to build some crafty interview questions and some very powerful narratives. You have some terrible narrative responses and some incredible narrative responses. But, you still struggle to make sense of it all.

How do you assess all of the information coming across your table? How do you create a scientific analysis of your search for the best workplace attitudes? You now have to get ready to do something with this information that makes sense for your committee. There is a way to assess candidates for their attitudes and dispositions, and this will be discussed in Chapter 5.

Thinking About Your Recruitment Process and Who Is Exempt

This chapter will examine your talent-search process and help you to understand who should have to respond to or construct narratives as an applicant to your school or district. You've already created real-life narratives that you want to use, and your selected writer has done a great job for your team. Before you unleash your narratives and start using them during portions of your recruiting and hiring process, you have to decide where in your hiring process you should use narratives to best match your goals.

Criteria First; Screening Second

Reviewing applications, résumés, cover letters, names of applicants, or any other document should be put on hold by the school or district until the interview committee meets and goes through a process to:

- identify the core beliefs of the organization (if not already known);
- determine what makes the open job vacancy unique to the school;
- decide what interview tools should be used for all levels of the *entire* process.

The recruitment, pre-interview, and formal interview levels are all important. According to 100 school and district leaders who were surveyed in 2010, one of the problems within the hiring process that is established by hiring committees is that they do not invest in working through the entire hiring process, together, as a collective group. Instead, it is usually the human resources director or personnel director who takes things through the initial phases/levels of the hiring process—only to then meet up with those who will formally meet a group of eight to ten candidates during the formal interview.

This saves time for schools and districts, yes, but it also excludes one major component: the importance of identifying the very specific attitudes or given scenarios which all interviewees are expected to display or wrestle with during the actual interview. These can challenge our preconceptions and reveal previously unseen differences between the candidates.

Time restraints are challenging aspects of carrying out a full hiring process and one of the biggest headaches for school personnel to manage. However, this book will outline exact timelines that the school districts used and provide some common sense shortcuts that were utilized to save time without discounting the importance of the entire process. Hiring educators and school staff was in the top 2% of the most important responsibilities within a school district, according to the responses gathered within this study's survey tool.

Screening Second; Post-Recruitment Third

Many refer to the hiring process in different ways, but I like to think of screening and "post-recruitment" (a new term) as two different levels of the process. The general word *recruitment* is simply when the position is open, and you put a call out for applicants.

Screening should be up to the interview committee after narratives are used for round one, and there is no interviewing at all at this point. It can simply involve inviting all the applicants to a centralized location, such as an auditorium or cafeteria, to engage in various tasks/tools set forth by the hiring committee, from which the committee decides who to progress to the next level. Alternatively, an even better way to gather lots of materials in a hurry can be to send all applicants blind carbon copy (Bcc) e-mails containing questions and narratives to be completed and returned by a certain expiration date.

Consider this situation: you need to hire a special education teacher at your middle school. How would you do it? What would be your process? What would be your criteria? Who would determine it? Would you set aside an entire day to establish criteria with your committee? Might you need only one hour?

Then suppose you received 20 formal application packets posted on an on-line application management software program set up by your district for the position of special education teacher. Could you invite all 20 applicants to your middle school cafeteria for further screening? Could they be screened using a 50-question survey and maybe two to three narrative tool essays that reflect your committee's established criteria for your school's next special education teacher? Or could you e-mail questions to candidates, or ask them to visit your website, set up an account and have all of their submitted information right at your fingertips within weeks?

For documentation purposes and for legal proactivity, since all candidates could be invited to attend or to respond to your next steps, you are giving everyone an opportunity to be successful. This is critically important and philosophically sound. No one person would be excluded from the start of the entire process. Could a complete stranger to the school and your colleague's friend be scientifically assessed on their knowledge, skills, beliefs, and attitudes for what it takes to be a great special education teacher at your middle school, both at the same time? Will the playing field be leveled within your organization? Do you wish to examine the attitudes of all applicants and then eliminate those attitudes which do not match the desired responses of your organization?

Could you provide one hour for your candidates to complete the survey instrument and narrative tasks, either on your time or their own time within the comfort of their own home? Is this too much time to invest? It is not worthy to investigate all aspects of a candidate for taxpayers and their children?

Screening all applicants will give you a thoroughness that will make you comfortable that you are not second-guessing those whom you invite to the next level—the "post-recruitment" phase. Post-recruitment is when you actually invite someone to an interview and is the result of any completed recruitment and screening process.

What if you calculate the results of your applicant surveys and narratives (which we will fully uncover in Chapter 6) and 18 applicants score in the top tier? What do you do? Do you interview all 18 out of the 20 applicants—or 50 out of 52 applicants? Some larger districts have hundreds of applicants. Would they interview 200 out of 323 applicants? Certainly not. You will have to determine the next steps of the process based on the number of applicants who scored favorably and their responses. But if you have 12 applicants who score wonderfully, then the committee should interview all 12.

If you have 50, then your assessment scale was not set up to narrow down your largest pools. I have not seen any screening process result in having more than 10% of the applicants score in the "desired" range in any of the districts using narrative theory and/or survey tools. Ten percent is certainly manageable. Your scale has to be worthy of sorting your applicants using various methods of screening.

The word "survey" is used because this is a commonly used tool for carrying out talent searches. It is important to establish a very high bar so you do not compromise the types of responses that you are looking for while staying true to what a high rating is versus a medium to low rating. Take the time to work out your survey or questionnaire measures—there are all sorts of resources out there to help you determine the best fit for your organization.

Narrative theory models provide an effective method of mining for all types of core features in your talent search. Remember, there is some science behind mining for attitudes and your scales and scoring will prove to be your friend, not the enemy.

Your process and results can be scientific, legal, creative, and worthy of what you want to find in a person who will lead your students to greatness. Do not think that you will be stuck. The tenets of education usually stay the same from place to place. We all focus on students, learning, achievement, and the culture of our schools. In this next section, I will outline a typical brain-storming session which your interview team should journey through together so you can examine what you *desire* in your school as you seek to find matching attitudes from those you will invite to a formal interview.

No One Is Exempt From Narrating Their Own Worlds

The Elm Grove and Gardenville school districts, which you will learn more about later, believe that the process of using narrative theory in their hiring techniques is good for anyone and everyone. Remember, attitudes need to be explored for all educators and staff members. No one should be exempt.

If your organization believes that there are best practices, proper attitudes about the workplace, things that you believe are "right," then stick to those elements and demand that your applicants fit into the mold of your organizational integrity and belief-system.

It is important to remember that the narrative process is not about hiring all the same robots, but rather more about canvassing for attitudes that are similar to those that you believe to be extremely important. As a result, you can move an organization forward, together, and not get hung up on the barriers of employees or naysayers who might spoil the excitement about school reform or school improvement.

You see, it is easy to bring others on board when they share the same beliefs and commitment to the organization. This isn't brainwashing. It is smart hiring. It is smart to want to locate attitudes that will stand the test of time. From Earl, the custodian, to Joanne, the cafeteria monitor, to Nancy, registered nurse, to Ron, a board member; everyone has a story to tell and everyone also has a story to respond to. It is crucial that your stories have content that is meaningful enough for you to extract the best, desired responses.

What About Library Media Specialists?

There is something to be said about looking more deeply at the humans who, allegedly, love kids and who will work with kids for 30 or more years. Dr. Peter Loeh reminded me of a librarian I knew while attending high school. Consider the story of Dawn below and notice how she viewed young adult students:

> Um, excuse me . . . yes, you with the red sweatshirt on . . . where is your student ID? You don't have your ID? You cannot get into the library without your ID. Why aren't you prepared? If you really wanted to get into the library, you would have brought your ID. So, I don't think you really want to be here or are looking to be focused if you didn't bring your ID in the first place. And . . . I think I told you to bring your ID yesterday, didn't I?
>
> *(Dawn, "The Mean" Librarian)*

Dawn would antagonize every student who did not have their ID to get into the library. "Where's your ID?" "You do not have your ID, so you do not have the opportunity to have books." I mean, it was ridiculous. She knew who my friend was. She saw him every day. The last thing I would think of doing is visiting a high school that I didn't attend just to steal their books or to openly set fire to the stacks.

Maybe Dawn wasn't mean when she was hired, or maybe Dawn became mean because of some life events that reshaped her happiness into meanness. I want to give Dawn the benefit of the doubt. But, maybe Dawn was mean even before she started working in a high school and maybe the people who hired Dawn could have explored security issues or library usage policies through narrative tools that went beyond Dawn's résumé, transcripts, and a 45-minute job interview. Maybe Dawn could answer the technical questions about the "librarianship," but maybe that was because she was only asked the technical questions about her skills and abilities during her interview that took place 30 years ago.

What About School Leaders?

School leaders, like library media specialists, are not exempt from storytelling or responding to stories. As I researched various school principals in New York State and asked them about their perceptions of high-stakes testing, I used narrative tools to draw out their responses.

Here are the tools that were used—these were created by three school leaders, prior to my two months of fieldwork:

Principal Narrative #1:

The Department Chair for English coordinates NY State ELA (English Language Arts) practice tests for all of the grade levels that have these tests. The students try different tests throughout the course of the year and these are found on the NY State Education website. Students need to practice, and teachers need to practice with their students. Familiarity with the test is so important. It's like knowing what China looks like before you visit it so there is no culture shock. That is why we dump money into buying test-prep books as we get ready for the "real test." Pre-testing is a necessity. They need to know where they stand before they take the actual ELA Assessment. The students and the teachers want to be able to write right in the books, but we need to keep them for students for future years since the test-prep books are pretty expensive. So, we are in a crunch right now with what to do. That seems to be a resource that everyone wants more of. And, since the tests have changed a little bit since all of the Grades 3–8 tests have been introduced, everyone wants to have more practice and try more examples that these books provide.

(Elise, Grades K–5 Elementary School Principal)

Principal Narrative #2:

I would say that I feel like I have a good grasp of what we are doing here at my school and what really matters: instruction and professional development, not tests. That, to me, is a good understanding of my leadership strengths . . . because I am focused on the child, not the tests. I am focused on the teachers, not the tests. Professional development is really up to the teachers, however. They select what they want to read and then we pay for it and order it for them. We have building-based reading groups, as well. If they want to attend out-of-building conferences or workshops, I pay for it out of my building budget. Last week, one of our ELA teachers went to a brain research workshop. I forget where it was or what it included. But, see, that is the stuff that really matters. The tests are not the focus. Good instruction is. And, it is different for every teacher. Each teacher's knowledge base and experience base is different, so while one might need some help in differentiated instruction, another might help in building writing strategies within the content area. That is the essence of professional development that I offer them. Anything goes.

(Sean, Grades 6–8 Middle School Principal)

Principal Narrative #3:

Professional development and the topic of high-stakes testing are not easy topics to uncover. It isn't clear-cut unless you work with your teachers to discuss explicitly what you believe, where you want to go, what attitude towards these assessments you want to have, and what the plan of attack is going to be. For example, I, point-blank, told my teachers that I do not believe in test-prep or drill and skill tactics. I told them that I was going to ban all purchases that this school used to make to the big publishers. That's it. Test-prep books were banned. A few teachers rebelled, but we laughed with each other about it and talked about getting rid of that comfort zone of using these books to drive instruction. I believe that the test format is a genre that we should teach, but not over a long period of time. It is something that needs to be treated as a genre study—just like poetry or non-fiction. Then, we looked at research on test-prep and formulaic writing and found that these methods gleaned no better results than having classrooms that focused on creative writing and critical-thinking skills. We talked about activities that elicit student-centered writing based on their oral language skills. Some teachers even went to workshops on linking oral language with authentic writing. We had a game plan!

(Ron, Grades 3–8 Intermediate School Principal)

These three narratives helped me to mine for an awful lot of information about school leaders' attitudes and their perceptions about the four SLAC creeds (students, learning, achievement, and culture) as they pertained to the topic of testing and assessments. If I had not used these narrative tools, the outcome of my interview sessions would have been dependent on the quality of my interview questions and nothing else. Narratives, in this case, helped me to have a starting point about the issues that needed to be uncovered a bit more—issues that I thought were important for leading schools within an accountability culture. I learned so much about these professionals' views of accountability leadership and high-stakes testing. Some had incredible attitudes and dispositions about testing and assessment; others did not give high quality responses at all.

It is important to remember the idea that if your committee has strong beliefs about something, such as testing and assessments, then narratives can be constructed to carry out your sense of organization, your sense of purpose and the integrity behind an issue that is non-negotiable for sustaining your positive culture. Some schools believe in test prep. Others don't. So, how do you distinguish the leaders who will lead you (or not lead you) through accountability initiatives regarding testing beliefs and philosophies? How do you distinguish between school leaders who have a laissez-faire professional development philosophy versus those who are more targeted and secure with organizational decision-making? Narratives expose those deeper attitudes that you never thought you could find. Until now.

Working Through Embellishment

How might we work with candidates who are embellishing their answers and responses during an interview process? How do we deal with any false perceptions that they display? I've asked myself this very same question when reviewing the narrative responses from candidates during my own recruitment and hiring processes and it becomes pretty clear as to whom is staying on target with your committee's desired responses and who isn't staying on target. The Elm Grove and Gardenville school districts have also successfully looked beyond embellishment trends.

What you have to start and end with, though, is the belief that no one is exempt from storytelling or responding to others' stories because through such a lens, you will be re-enacting their deepest thoughts, desires, and workplace attitudes. It is the story that makes us more human and we need to pick apart and understand all of the "humanness" in our bus drivers, crossing guards, principals, superintendents, board members, and even parent volunteers. What it will take is a little more time and energy to craft narratives for these people to review and respond to, but the lasting effect will be a smarter hiring result that was ingrained in a thoughtful, inclusive talent search.

Most of the narratives created by educational professionals were very specific and very targeted in terms of what the most desirable responses should include. However, we all have a story to tell and we tell our stories with expression at parties, work, or anywhere. It is probably impossible to exclude dramatic embellishments that might surface during face-to-face discussions with others, but that is OK. You would be using narratives to supplement your other screening tools and interviews and examining all multiple measures together in order to see if everything is consistent.

Not many candidates go way beyond the parameters of what a committee would like to hear from them regarding narratives. However, individuals do exist who come up short and do not fully convey what they are feeling about a scenario of a narrative example. This could be due to nervousness or a lack of confidence. No one will ever truly know. The Elm Grove and Gardenville school districts did not have many candidates who tried to provide more than the committee wanted. It is the craft of using narratives that will assist you in finding candidates who are more sincere versus those who are not aligned with your ideals. In those respects, you can always follow up with questions in order to clarify your points.

Assessing Candidates for Attitudes and Dispositions

I remember hiring Sheila . . . and boy, she gave great answers during the interview. That was two years ago. Her knowledge of science was awesome! She spoke very eloquently, had some experience from another school district, but then something started to happen to her. She became disengaged. She didn't seem to fit in any longer at our school or maybe she didn't want to fit in. We started to implement some changes to our master schedule . . . block scheduling, you know . . . and Sheila just didn't cooperate. I wished we asked her about it during her interview. I wished I gauged her on the changes that we as a school were going through. She hated it and her students hated it because she hated it. Discipline increased as a result. Sheila was not on board. She thought it was too long to stay with the same class for 90 minutes. She barely had enough activities for the kids to travel through her science class. She was a major thorn in the school's side because she would dismiss her kids after about 80 minutes and they would stand in the hall waiting for their next class to finish up. When I say this I really mean it: we at Washington Middle School really bought into the need for block scheduling except for one person: Sheila. She requested a transfer last month and probably won't get it because she is non-tenured and I feel that her lack of cooperation needs to be handled by our human resources department. It is so sad. I really like her, but I don't like how she fights the system because she doesn't like something that we all feel is working out wonderfully. Our students' achievement improved by 37%. I wish I could turn back the clock to two years ago. I wish I could have almost measured her lack of cooperation then.

(John Owens, Principal)

Washington Middle School weren't looking for a robot. They weren't looking for someone to brainwash. This is a classic case of an organization whose hiring practices were centered around knowledge, skills, and

Assessing Attitudes and Dispositions

abilities, only. Washington Middle School did not mine for attitudes—especially attitudes that would have been exposed before their block scheduling initiatives began.

Washington Middle School could have created a narrative tool to use during their interview sessions. This would have been based on the block-scheduling scenario, along with other topics that they would ultimately face at their school. The narrative could have been written as a non-biased, first-person position on the topic so candidates would not be led to agree with block scheduling and encouraged to let their true feelings came out. Maybe Washington Middle School could have created something like this:

> Jacobs Middle School moved to a block schedule format last year. I'm not sure what I think about it for our school, but there are pros and cons to everything, I guess.
>
> I mean . . . having the students for two class periods in a row? Wow . . . that takes a lot of prep work and energy. I would have to really re-think my teaching. On the other hand, sometimes one class period isn't enough time to get my students situated or have them accomplish everything that they need to complete. I dunno . . . it is such a complex topic . . . maybe we should just wait to see what happens next year at Jacobs . . . or maybe we should jump right in and try it. Either way, we have to come to a decision regarding block scheduling before the schedule is created and students receive their schedules over the summer.
>
> (Ron Gladstone, Washington Middle School Social Studies Teacher)

This narrative tool has the power to uncover human attitudes about block scheduling by situating the speaker to respond, authentically. It presents the topic of block scheduling and a few opposing positions through the thoughts and reflections of Ron. These give readers two possible avenues to entertain: the candidates being interviewed would have to either like it or not like it and detail their position in writing. It also touches upon the idea of "someone needing to make a decision," which gets to the heart of how collective decisions in an organization might either upset or not affect the candidate being interviewed. Perhaps this narrative only needs a simple direction placed at the top of it: "In no less than 150 words, please respond to whatever you feel is important in this narrative—which was written by one of your potential future colleagues."

The narrative is non-biased, indeed, but it will open up emotional responses based on the use of this human tool. To ask an interview question about block scheduling will not give you the same "way in" to the specific dispositions of the candidate. Sure, one can simply ask, "How do you feel about block scheduling?" but many other points might be forgotten by the respondent.

Instead, as we read stories, from a real person, about real topics, using real language, we are compelled as humans to take a position, wrestle with it, and as we explain our thoughts, we are left with insights about our own true passions regarding the issues.

What if Sheila had been able to provide her true feelings about block scheduling *before* she was hired? What if other high quality candidates had the same forward thinking and philosophy about block scheduling that Washington Middle School desired? Would they be better teachers than Sheila? Would it even matter?

It does matter. Dealing with a difficult employee is one of the worst problems to have when going to work. Remember, there are hundreds, thousands of candidates out there competing for educational positions. You have to find the best match for your organization without stifling creativity and freewill. You wouldn't base your entire interview on this one narrative sample, but it certainly would help. Remember, using narrative tools should be a cultural and consistent process for your school or district that is relevant and customized to your institution.

Using one narrative is fine, because it might expose some of the attitudes that you definitely do not want in your hires, but it might also be a bit unfair to use only one sample tool. The Elm Grove and Gardenville school districts used narratives throughout their entire screening and post-recruitment process. They also used narratives during their interview process by inviting candidates to the interview 15 minutes prior to meeting their committee. The narrative tool that was created for Washington Middle School was used to illustrate a point: narratives can pack a punch and dig deeper for what you are dying to know about your candidates. It wouldn't be used to determine the ultimate fate of the entire hiring process.

Assessing Attitudes and Dispositions

Many educators advocate the use of multiple narrative tools at multiple levels of the hiring process. But, one major problem exists. How do we judge everything? How do we assess responses? How do we evaluate emotions and dispositions? How do we sift through human responses to get to our desired results? How complex does it have to be? How do we keep track of everything? Where do we begin? Let's start with an exercise about "love."

Designing Rubrics

Think about measuring "love" for a minute. Think about your spouse or significant other and brainstorm all the characteristics, actions, and qualities that go into your definition of his or her love for you. Think this through: what do you believe can be measured? Can love be quantified? It depends on what you do to create a process that will be as objective as possible when assessing human attitudes and dispositions.

We already measure the knowledge, skills, and abilities of our candidates through rating scales and rubrics, so why can't narratives also have scales, rubrics, and scoring charts, as well? We have all seen various types of checklists for scoring an interviewee's survey answers at an interview. Some use a 1–2–3–4 scale; others use a 1–3–5–7 or a 1–10 scale. Some use letter grades. Some use checklists. According to some of my previous work regarding how to assess various candidates' own authored stories or responses to narrative stories, a rubric system that is clear and precise at all levels needs to be planned out ahead of time and revised to fit the new job vacancy.

If you have established the criteria with your committee and stick with those criteria throughout your entire talent search process, you have already created the evaluation tools for your narratives even before you write your narratives. Remember, everything has to be consistent and you already know the desired answers that your committee is seeking.

Let's go back to the example about love. What are some of the qualifiers for measuring love, if it can truly be measured? Let's say that the following descriptors provide a well-rounded, measurable, and human set of factors about love:

- expressions of love (affection, hugging, kissing, etc.)
- acts of love (helping, assisting, supporting, cooking, gift-giving, etc.)
- thoughtfulness about love (remembering, reminiscing, etc.).

There are probably thousands of ways to characterize love, and it will be different for everyone based on their own experiences and desires. But, what if we can get a group of people together and get them to agree on the top five characteristics of love? Well, what you have then is an agreed upon foundation for assessing love, and all you have to do is create a tool to assess love in a very easy, user-friendly way. Let's look at two examples (affection and support) from the list above in order to illustrate the point that almost everything can be measured using a rubric-based tool. Maybe you might use something that is outlined in Table 6.1.

Within your definition of "perfect affection," you decide that affection has to fit in to the following categories:

- duration and frequency (monthly, weekly, daily)
- contextual appropriateness (public versus private)
- satisfaction.

Within your definition of "perfect support," you decide support must be judged on the:

- quality of listening skills (engagement)
- ability to validate feelings
- effort to offer suggestions or come up with solutions together.

If a spouse or significant other does not meet these criteria, they would receive a low score on a 0–1–2–3 scale and a total score can, ultimately, be given—not that I would do this for measuring love in my own life, however! Notice the variance of language (in bold print) used within this rubric to tabulate or "score" the differences in each numerical level. Words, such as "no," "rarely," "often," "may," "usually," "almost," "not," "sometimes," and many other adverbial descriptors will help you to create

Assessing Attitudes and Dispositions

Table 6.1

Signs of Love	0	1	2	3
1. Affection	Shows **no** sign of satisfying affection in public or in private and affection **rarely** takes place within a month.	Affection is minimal (weekly) and it **often** does not satisfy my needs. It **may** also be inappropriate within the context when given.	Affection is **usually** satisfying, **almost** daily, and is **rarely** inappropriate according to the context.	**Shows** satisfying affection on a daily basis and **discerns** the difference between appropriate public and private affection.
2. Support	Does **not** appear to listen, make me feel better, or offer any suggestions or solutions to solve my issue.	**Appears** to listen, care, or says **something** to help me feel better when resolving my issue.	Listens well, verbally supports or touches me (hug, etc.) in a supportive manner, and **responds** to my issue with some type of suggestion or solution.	**Engaged and attentive** to the issue, offers **caring** support in a physical or verbal manner, and **strives to problem-solve with me.**

levels of degree. Charlotte Danielson's framework for teaching (2007) has been a historical model for rubric design. While converting "love" into this kind of rubric-based language seems creepy, it can be done. While interview teams will not measure love, they will measure elements that are important to them, such as block scheduling, student safety, anti-bullying programs, the effectiveness of student learning objectives (SLOs), and so much more.

We use rubrics to assess our students' writing, and we use rubrics to assess our teachers' and school leaders' performance through Annual Professional Performance Reviews (APPR). We can also use targeted rubrics aligned with our narrative tools and previously established criteria to evaluate our candidates. Attitudes and dispositions can be identified and ranked according to their responses as we then move ahead to determine which candidate is the best candidate according to narrative models. Attitudes and dispositions can be identified and ranked according to the responses that you receive.

Deciding on an Ideal Response to a Story: Establishing a Benchmark Narrative

Let's go back to the example about Washington Middle School and the desired response, supporting block scheduling. What are some characteristics that a committee might look for in a candidate's attitudes about block scheduling and the process for supporting the initiative? Let's say that the committee wishes to have the following workplace attitudes about block scheduling, based on Ron's non-biased narrative.

- Attitudes that only support block scheduling.
- Attitudes that recognize the need for thoughtful lesson planning and prep work to cover 90 minutes.
- Attitudes that only display the need for an energetic teacher in making block scheduling successful.
- Attitudes that demonstrate a commitment to reflecting on teaching practices within a block schedule.
- Attitudes that only support collaboration with other staff members to make the block scheduling initiative actually work.

These are known as your "benchmark criteria responses." Remember, you brainstormed your four SLAC creeds and decided that block scheduling was an issue about learning and achievement that your committee desired to uncover during their interviews. It is powerful to create the most-desired-response tool to match your narrative tool—this will give you a well-articulated response to validate your work and your rating and ranking of your candidates' responses. You have to always keep in mind what you desire and what you will discard within your process. There will be answers your team judges to be correct and there will be those that will be incorrect, even though the responses are genuine opinions and feelings from your candidates regarding many differing viewpoints about block scheduling. Responses will either fail to fit into your organizational beliefs, or they will greatly match what you need from your new team member in order to move forward and minimize resistance.

Earlier, we looked at a benchmark response in a rubric for defining "love." An ideal was created with characteristics of love and benchmark responses that would make many people happy about someone's attitudes about love. Many differing responses will exist—especially if you ask a candidate to write their own story—which is sometimes a nice way to open up a blank canvas for painting whatever picture that a candidate wants to communicate. But, even those types of tasks have a desired response that will match your desired benchmark criteria. Let me illustrate two benchmark stories to further our exploration of Washington Middle School's block scheduling topic.

First, let's look at a desired benchmark response. Then, we can review a story based on a quasi-committee's desire to have a candidate start from scratch without any pre-written leads. The differences between using two different tools (writing to respond or writing to explore) might get you two different narrative outcomes, but both types of narrative tasks should be aligned with your desired responses. Following is a response to the previous narrative example that illustrates the benchmark of a desired response according to Table 6.2.

Here, notice the attention to building a benchmark that covers all of the important issues that you would hope a candidate can carry out in his or her responses and that are most desired by your committee. The candidate touches upon almost every benchmark response and even goes a step further to talk about data collection—something that wasn't even an initial qualifier for Washington Middle School's consideration.

Again, thinking about the ideal will give you a sense of how to compare others' narratives to this, and this method goes far beyond the reaches of résumé and transcript analysis. Attitudes that are energetic, supportive of block scheduling, supportive of the decision-making process, and knowledgeable about reflection certainly are much better than an undesired response about not supporting block scheduling, being on the fence about the topic, not honoring the decision, or questioning block scheduling with an analysis about the cons of such a scheduling model. These attitudes would not match the attitudes that you wish to have at Washington Middle School. Such a process can assist your final hiring decision.

Assessing Attitudes and Dispositions

Table 6.2

Directions: In no less than 150 words, please provide a response to this narrative including any issue from the narrative that you feel is important. Please use proper conventions of writing, as you will be judged not only on the content that you provide but also on your command of proper written English.

Although Ron seems confused about what to do or think regarding block scheduling, the power that block scheduling can hold for students excites me! Ron truly is already in touch with the pros about block scheduling—getting kids situated, organized, and ready to work and complete tasks without interruption. For some, block scheduling might be "scary" because you have to plan for multiple activities, multiple differentiations, and think through your extended time for kids and how it is going to look for 90 minutes. I love collaborating with teachers so that block scheduling is comprehensive and interdisciplinary. Teaching is a craft and learning needs time to flourish. I support block scheduling and there is research to prove its effects for kids' learning.

Finally, the decision of the school is to make the best-informed decision and move it forward while also tracking the success of a program to see if there are lasting effects. I would also be excited to compile data about block scheduling and compare it with achievement outcomes from the old schedule. Extra time to complete writing tasks with the new Common Core Standards will give students the most successful shot at becoming their very best, taking pride in their work, and shaping their writing into solid revised and edited pieces!

Now, look at a benchmark narrative that was designed from scratch, as illustrated in Table 6.3. Again, this shows the ideal response that is used as a model benchmark, not a sample of how candidates must answer this question.

Creating benchmark responses gives you a conscious, concrete example that will help you to place scores into your rubrics. It will also help to reassure you that you are being as objective as possible with the 10 or 12 finalists who have already been already identified through the screening and post-recruitment process.

While this narrative process demands more creativity from the candidate who must produce a writing piece or a story about their position, much can be learned from the ingredients embedded within this benchmark. Narratives give humans the power to bring forth their own attitudes and dispositions about a topic. They give humans the chance to reflect and refract from others' responses, as well.

Table 6.3

Directions: In no less than 150 words, please write a story as if you are a teacher who started working in a school that moved to a block schedule format. In your story, write as if you are the teacher, in 1st person. Be sure to express your attitudes about block scheduling in some way—whether you agree or disagree with the new scheduling model. Please use proper conventions of writing, as you will be judged not only on the content and attitudes that you provide, but also on your command of proper written English.
I was scared at first. I mean, I was moving from five 40-minute blocks to a longer every-other-day model with chunks of 90+ minutes (with the same students seated in front of me) to work on their social studies writing. When I think about all of the gains that my students have made, I wouldn't have it any other way. Johnny, one of my most challenging students, actually needed time to write. What once frustrated him within a short class period turned out to be the best thing possible for him. I loved talking with the ELA teacher about the writing process and craft of writing so I could use the same consistent features in my classroom. I even team-taught with the ELA teacher so the kids saw the consistency with what we were asking them to do. That was not only collaboration, but it was intensive teamwork. We both saw a metamorphosis in the students' writing. They had a sort of fresh stamina when they were writing. They tackled longer pieces with confidence and it was all because they were given time by the new school structure of being involved in block scheduling. I was no longer scared, but rather a teacher who professionally advanced myself, and saw the power, first-hand, with how the students ultimately did on their writing pieces.

    The same benchmark criteria supporting block scheduling were covered in this example, and while all candidates' stories might not include all of the desired qualities, narrative analysis will help you to weed through and select those whose responses or stories are more desired than others. All of a sudden, a candidate becomes more "humanized" by writing in the first person while they either support or refute your desired initiatives. It is exciting to know your candidates more intimately in this way, and you can feel better about selecting the very best school staff member in whom you are investing over $2 million for the balance of a successful career.

    This non-biased narrative option gave Washington Middle School responses from their pool of candidates that ranged from desired to not desired (with lots of other responses in between). You have the power to question and assess each candidate's responses so that you gain insight into their attitudes. But, you must first establish your criteria, stick to it, and create benchmark responses; next, you must create the narratives that you feel are exemplary for comparing others' responses, and then ultimately use rubric-based tools to objectively insert the results of the candidates. What may seem like a long process really is not, and it is worth every minute to know what others think, what others believe, and how others value what you may value. Later, in Chapter 7, I will analyze the time on task for including a narrative process into your recruitment and hiring practices. Until then, let's look carefully at two narratives, putting them side by side in order to make sense of them through rubric-based designs.

A Comparative Analysis of Narratives: One Example

At this point, it is important to demonstrate how three different narratives can be compared and then framed to fit within a rubric that was designed to align itself with the original narrative task. You will be able to take the previous examples used in this chapter one step further and actually see how objectivity will become your friend, not foe. Later, you will see some of the narrative tools used by the Elm Grove and Gardenville school districts and the responses that they were able to glean from their wonderful experiences, but you will also have a glimpse into practicing and thinking about how this craft can fit into your organization very easily.

First, let us establish the topic through a narrative used at Morehead Elementary School, which includes their benchmark responses, and then the ideal benchmark narrative response. All of these tools are placed together in Table 6.4.

Morehead believes that there is a difference in what a child can do and loves to do and that there is something to be said about the role of motivation and pushing kids to higher levels. They also believe that there needs to be a certain type of flexibility when looking at multiple measures of diagnosing student achievement and enrichment potentialities. Finally, Morehead knows that a calm initial response along with professional handling of further discussions to balance the needs of staff and parents is what is best for Olivia. The narrative task and benchmark story were constructed by Morehead and such a narrative worked extremely well. Comparing the responses called for an objective assessment of the qualities of the attitudes

Table 6.4

Background: A gifted and talented (GT) teacher retired at Morehead Elementary School (a small school in the eastern part of New York State, and a committee was assembled to hire a new teacher. The committee consisted of eight individuals ranging from the principal to teacher representatives to a parent and student representative. The committee brainstormed the four SLAC creeds and decided that four major topics for the GT teacher would need to be presented through narratives. Three of those topics were presented to candidates during a screening process where over 80 applicants showed an interest in the position. All 80 applicants were sent an e-mail blast with directions for carrying out two interview tools: narrative responses and a small survey about best practices in teaching high ability students.

Three narratives were given to the candidates, and they all had time to complete the three tasks. Rubrics assessed the responses of the 42 candidates who replied by the due date. As a result, 12 finalists were recruited for a longer interview process which also included one narrative that candidates were responsible for writing about before their scheduled interview. The committee interviewed the final six candidates over a two-day span. Here is an exact copy of the final interview narrative used by Morehead Elementary School:

Directions: Read the following story and please respond/react in no more than 200 words regarding your feelings, professional opinions, values, or recommendations. You can imagine that this parent said this to you while you were trying to supervise children during bus duty. What will you say to this parent and how will you handle being caught off guard during bus duty? Please be sure to also pay attention to the conventions of using proper written English:

My daughter comes home bored with school every single day. She is not challenged in the classroom at all. She is so depressed about school and I want to know why she wasn't accepted into GT this year. I mean . . . what a slap in the face . . . such a bright kid . . . but not allowed to be in GT? I've been talking to lots of other parents and they are equally upset that their kids are not in GT, either. I'm thinking of looking at other schools for her. Why are some kids, who are not as smart as my daughter, allowed to be in GT and what are you doing with her regular classroom teacher to help my daughter not become so bored each day? This is just ridiculous. All she does is cry when she comes home.

(Mrs. Wehrle, Grade 4 Parent)

The benchmark responses desired by the Morehead hiring committee included attitudes which supported:

- being able to handle parent complaints *professionally*
- knowing about the *attitudes of the selection process* that would be used by the GT Teacher

Assessing Attitudes and Dispositions

- *collaboration* plans with the classroom teacher
- doing the best thing for the child and not the adults in the school (but, being flexible).

The benchmark narrative response that captures these benchmark responses and presents the most ideal candidate would look like this:

Mrs. Wehrle, I would be happy to talk with you after I take my bus line outside. Can we meet in Room 107 in five minutes? I hope you can stay, as I have some ideas that I think will help.

After bus duty: I have been thinking about your daughter, Olivia, since we gave the teachers and Olivia a questionnaire about her love of science (our next block of GT) and checked her scores on her latest science assessment and benchmark unit tests. It appears that she loves science, but does not do well on the actual assessments. Would you agree? So, I have been thinking, I would like to see what Olivia can and cannot do in a few initial sessions of GT pull-out so I can see if she will be able to attend GT while doing well in her classroom work. I will provide her teacher, Mrs. Davis, with some options for getting Olivia to perform at her very best in class, and I think it would be a good idea if we all sat down with Olivia to explain to her that this is on a trial-basis only. I would hate for her to be bored in school and end up hating school. She is such a neat kid and I would hate for her to come home crying because she is disengaged from us!

that would surface within the narratives. Therefore, Table 6.5 and Table 6.6 represent the rubrics that were used to assess these four benchmark responses/themes that Morehead insisted are present in their finalists' work.

As you can see in Table 6.5, a rubric was then created by Morehead to match the benchmark responses that range from least desired to most desired. A total score of 12 would come from a candidate who represented Morehead's ideal attitudes regarding an example or role that their typical gifted and talented (GT) teacher might experience at their school.

Here is the collection of themes that Morehead considered as they searched for workplace attitudes within their candidates. Notice the levels of language within this rubric and the specific expectations that Morehead established according to Table 6.5.

As a side note, it is also worth mentioning that while it is best practice to share rubrics before someone carries out their work (we strive to do this for our students so they know what type and quality of work we are looking for), it is not appropriate to share any benchmark response rubrics with your candidates-for-hire. They would reveal all of your secrets!

Table 6.5

Themes	0	1	2	3
1. Professional handling of situation.	Either ignores, acts rudely, or defers responsibility to the classroom teacher.	Appears to only appease parent or reserves discussion for a later date/time.	Tries to have private discussion within context due to the nature of the parent's demeanor.	De-escalates situation from taking place in an inappropriate location/context while presenting rational problem-solving outcomes.
2. Noble attitudes about selection process (flexibility).	Shows no signs of flexible outcomes.	Places responsibility on parent and child for proving that child should be given chance to demonstrate GT work.	Places responsibility on the school for further investigating pursued GT inclusion.	Offers chance for student to demonstrate talents without promise of formal long-range GT instruction.
3. Collaboration efforts are presented.	Does not problem-solve to include teacher or child in any way.	Offers suggestions for talking with teacher only about the complaint.	Discusses plans for meeting and collaborating with teacher to come up with best possible solution.	Initiates an exact plan of what the collaboration efforts will entail for parent, teacher, and child.
4. Child (not adults) first.	Shows no interest in child's feelings or perceptions of the situation. Believes that teachers have made decision for what is best and will stick with decision without recognizing child's world.	Validates child's feelings, but only through parent's complaint.	Empathizes with child's feelings.	Supports child through positive comments about ability and recognizes the importance of child's inclusion in the plan of action.

Table 6.6

Conventions of English	0	1	2	3
1. Grammar and sentence structure.	Many grammatical errors (more than 4) exist and/or sentence fragments or incomplete sentences are apparent.	Some grammatical errors (3–4) exist and/or sentence fragments or incomplete sentences are apparent.	Few grammatical errors (1–2) exist and/or sentence fragments or incomplete sentences may be apparent.	Sentence and grammar structures balance simple, compound, and complex sentence types. Writing is clear, focused, and creative all at the same time.
2. Spelling.	Many spelling mistakes (more than 4) exist either with difficult words or the possibility of careless spelling outcomes.	Some spelling mistakes (3–4) exist either with difficult words or the possibility of careless spelling outcomes.	Few spelling mistakes (1–2) exist either with difficult words or the possibility of careless spelling outcomes.	Expert spelling techniques are apparent and higher-level vocabulary is used and not misspelled.
3. Punctuation.	Many errors (more than 4) exist using common punctuation standards.	Some errors (3–4) exist using common punctuation standards.	Few errors (1–2) exist using common punctuation standards.	Punctuation is used to capture narrative tone and/or effective punctuation is used to exemplify feelings and attitudes.

Interview committees may, however, decide to share their "conventions of English" rubric with candidates or finalists before they carry out their work.

Table 6.6 shows a sample of such a rubric created by Morehead on English usage. This could certainly be used by any other school when carrying out a collective tabulation of a final raw score, both for the task of responding to a narrative and for candidates asked to create their own story.

Now let's get to the actual comparison of two authored narratives by two separate candidates (Terri and Jennifer) who were finalists up to this point. Both fared extremely well during the screening process, interview process, and examination of all application documents used to apply for the position of Elementary School GT teacher. In Tables 6.7 and 6.8, you will find their responses to the narrative and directions in Table 6.4.

Weighing in: Aligning the Multiple Measures of Hiring the "Best"

Jennifer, Morehead's Candidate #2, will not necessarily "get the job" if this one narrative scores better than the other candidate's. What it will do, however, is create a lens into the attitudes of the individuals and how

Table 6.7

> *Mrs. Wehrle, as you report how your daughter is feeling, I want to reassure you that we will try our best to look at all of the evidence that we have used to make a decision about GT. Please know that I will meet with her teacher to go over a plan to try and help your daughter become more challenged in class. If she is successful in that, we can certainly re-evaluate her status for GT and if you wish, you can call me for an update or I can call you (either way).*
>
> *I want to take this very seriously and I promise that we can look at this further. Can you give me two days to meet with her teacher and gather more information? We can even share with you the actual identification documents and assessments that we used to come to our decision, so you can see, first-hand, why we made our decision. I would be glad to show you that and I could also meet with your daughter to show her everything that we used to make our decision. It might help her to better understand everything.*
>
> *(Terri, Candidate #1)*

Assessing Attitudes and Dispositions

Table 6.8

> Hi Mrs. Wehrle! Wait. Just give me one second to get another adult to take over my bus line. I see Mr. Peterson over there and I think he can help out so we can talk.
>
> I am so sorry that you are upset and if Olivia is feeling this way . . . gosh . . . . I wouldn't want to come to school either if I were her. But, wait . . . let's sit in the Cafeteria across the hall so we can talk privately. I remember assessing Olivia's thoughts on a potential science pull-out unit that I was going to use on forensic science. Her answers to the questionnaire I gave to all higher ability and moderate ability 4th graders showed that she didn't really want to be in this GT unit.
>
> However, maybe she didn't know much about what we would be doing and then maybe she heard her friends talking about how cool it is? Who knows? You know how kids are, right? Anyway, I used those questionnaires and looked at each child's science performance and academic progress in non-fiction reading and writing, since forensic science is very technical. I don't recall how Olivia rated on that assessment off hand, but can we meet tomorrow to go over it.
>
> We should also sit down with Olivia and her teacher to see if she could try it out a little bit to get a feel for it if we all agree that she should at least try it. I'm all for challenging kids if they are doing what they should be doing in class already, and I know Olivia is a great student! After that, maybe we should visit Miss Watkins (our school Social Worker) just to make sure that Olivia isn't feeling down in the dumps about anything else. You never know, Mrs. Wehrle . . . sometimes kids keep other things inside and this would be a good thing to do (just to be sure). So, let's talk tomorrow at 12:00 during my planning period. What phone number can I reach you?
>
> (Jennifer, Candidate # 2)

their beliefs align with those of Morehead, even if there isn't a "perfect score" in all of the desired attitudes. Narrative theory, while it is an art and science, should never be the only measure used to determine final decisions. Narrative theory should be used to enter into new areas of educators' dispositions and hearts—which have often been ignored during regular traditional interviews. As we continue to analyze this one example, we learn an awful lot about Terri and Jennifer—beliefs about issues that we didn't know before. Morehead established a wonderful task which received incredible results.

In this case, although Terri's response is mostly appropriate, there is a huge difference between Terri and Jennifer's narratives. The length of the narratives often gives little insight into the quality of the narratives—even though in this case Jennifer's narrative is much longer.

Terri met the established criteria from the directions of "writing no more than 200 words" in her response, so a candidate should never be perceived to have better SLAC creed attitudes just because the narrative appears to have a longer response. I have seen long narratives which were empty and shallow in content, and I have seen shorter narratives pack a punch and match a school district's desired benchmark response. We see variance in both student and adult written work.

The application documents that Terri and Jennifer submitted were exemplary; the interviews for both candidates were solid—they also included questions about the attitudes of the teachers ranging from assessments, homework policies, community involvement, literacy best practices, and even communication patterns that a principal might appreciate from a teacher.

Both Terri and Jennifer were good writers with few to no errors in written expression or conventions, but the variation in narrative content is huge for so many reasons—you could almost feel the differences in tone and content. At one point, Morehead committee members realized that Terri only stated how Olivia was feeling through the eyes of her mom. As you look at Terri's narrative more carefully, you notice she doesn't actually write Olivia's name—not even once. The narrative seems cold and stuck on a procedural handling of Mrs. Wehrle's complaint—even though, for the most part, the complaint is appropriately handled.

Jennifer goes so far as to recommend social worker intervention (as a proactive measure—which is also something that Morehead did not include in their exemplary benchmark narrative, but enjoyed reading). So, in this case, Jennifer went above and beyond the Morehead expectations and problem-solving rationale. This further defined the thought process about Jennifer's deeper love and care of children.

Jennifer's narrative was incredibly thorough, and she showed a deep flexibility for a student who was obviously upset and maybe not challenged to her fullest ability. Jennifer demonstrated her attitudes about the identification process for GT and showed us that she would use questionnaires to

Assessing Attitudes and Dispositions

supply further information by gathering students' perceptions about future units of study and students' interest levels in those units of study.

As multiple measures are crucial in determining the outcome of the interview process, there is much to be said about the differences between Terri and Jennifer's narrative responses. In Table 6.9, you will see how the Morehead interview committee assessed the narratives authored by Terri and Jennifer.

Narrative methods provide an additional measure to the selection process and may not always be the deciding factor. In this case, however, as shown in Table 6.9, there is a clear distinction between Terri, with a score of 18, and Jennifer, with a score of 24.

Jennifer's narrative not only set her apart from Terri, but also taught the interview committee and staff at large a valuable lesson. Jennifer's narrative was actually a deciding factor for whom to hire, and even though Jennifer

Table 6.9

Rubric Topic Number for Benchmark Response Content	Terri's Scored Results	Jennifer's Scored Results
1	2	3
2	2	3
3	2	3
4	1	3
Total	7	12
Rubric Topic Number for Conventions	**Terri's Scored Results**	**Jennifer's Scored Results**
1	3	3
2	3	3
3	3	3
4	2	3
Total	11	12
Overall Total	**18**	**24**

did end up getting the job as Morehead's new GT teacher, Jennifer's narrative went on to do something more for the Morehead interview committee and staff, as you will see. But remember, using narrative methods brings about an additional multiple measure for the overall experience that an interview team has with any particular candidate. The scores of 18 and 24 do not exclusively point to whom Moorehead should have hired, but these scores do reveal something very unique between both of the final applicants.

Narrative as a Learning Tool for All: Reflection and Professional Development

Patricia, the Morehead Elementary School Principal, who was part of the interview committee for finding a new GT teacher, was amazed by the narrative process that she facilitated for her committee. Look at her reflections about the screening process, working with her committee, interviewing, and then ultimately being able to hire Jennifer:

> *I never would have known ... I mean, I never would have known what Terri and Jennifer were really thinking about with the scenario that we gave them if we hadn't looked at their attitudes and responses carefully. You cannot possibly imagine what this whole process did for our committee and school. In the past, I usually just led an interview team to interview about six to eight candidates who appeared to be the most qualified candidates on paper, and then we would create about 12 questions about our school and teaching, in general, and then just end up rating them and ranking them on a big board. To engage in using stories to figure out how a teacher feels and would truly handle something ... to see how they perceive a situation and problem-solve — it is a priceless event that our candidates went through. Don't get me wrong ... from the start ... it was a lot of work. The more we engage in creating narratives for our talent searches, the timelier we will be, as well. The whole narrative creation and assessment process added about two hours to our usual eight hours of creating questions and interviewing a small*

pool of finalists, but it did something more than just open up my eyes about the attitudes of a candidate. It did something more for the committee. We learned together. We shared such amazing discussions about what we believe, what we don't believe, and what we wish we could do in the future . . . you know . . . how we want our school to be . . . how we always desire to treat kids and parents. You have no idea how Jennifer has not only been one of the best teachers whom we have hired, but she has helped my staff to grow! You know . . . I shared her narrative with the entire staff after she was hired. We all talked about it. We all learned from it. I saw my entire staff not only believing in what we already know and do . . . but what we always could do to be better. To brainstorm criteria before screening and interviewing was new to me. I feel like I am a better leader because of just one small part that has been missing in my talent searches: to create a simple story.

(Patricia, Principal)

Being on an interview team is a form of professional development. Talking about a vision through the lens of what you will do to hire your next staff member is a form of intentional leadership and development. Stories push us to learn. Stories push us to share and bend our thoughts into something that assists our own identity-in-practice and renovation of not only our professional "selves," but our personal "selves."

Patricia used various narratives during her faculty meetings and grade level meetings to evoke emotion from her staff. She used stories to formulate her thematic professional development in-service workshops that kept the focus on Morehead's school-wide vision. She delved into something that she never did before: use narratives to go beyond her résumés, transcripts, and reference letters. Her search for attitudes will drive her future staffing decisions and professional development planning for her entire staff.

But, Patricia and her staff were not the only ones to learn from using stories within her interview process. Jennifer learned. Terri learned. These narratives impacted every applicant who moved through the Moorhead recruitment and interview phases. Notice what Jennifer said about her experience of entering into the Morehead final interview session.

Assessing Attitudes and Dispositions

> *I got to the school and was so nervous. My palms were sweating and I was only obsessed with thinking about hoping to not have sweaty palms when I shook everyone's hand on the committee. It was so silly. I'm an adult who doesn't have stage fright, but I was so nervous. And then . . . I go into a room before my interview and have to tackle another narrative. I thought to myself . . . boy, these people are intense! I already completed a few narratives in the initial stage of the process and I saw another one before my final interview. I'm glad I brought a pen! Anyway . . . I sat down and read the story about Olivia. I felt so sad for her and her mom—who, in my opinion, was only dealing with a crying child at home without having any of the facts about the GT program. So, I just wrote about what I would really do if I had to deal with that exact situation. I wasn't even thinking about whether my written response was 'right' or 'wrong.' I was only flushing out my feelings . . . my problem-solving tools . . . and when I read everything over after I wrote it all down . . . I thought . . . yeah . . . this is how I would hope my child's teacher would handle this situation if I were Mrs. Wehrle.*
>
> (Jennifer Watkins, GT Teacher)

Notice the feelings that are exhibited by Jennifer when she describes her experience. Relational reflections govern the embedded emotions of this narrative. Such a response brings us to the realization that stories truly work. They are close to our hearts.

You most likely have not mined for attitudes in your workplace by using narrative theory in this manner, and you most likely have not experienced the effects that narrative theory can have, not only for determining a candidate for hire, but for helping your organization to understand itself more as it continues to grow collectively and professionally. It can be a win-win for all. But, you still need to hear a few more success stories. You need to have more "proof," other than the schools that have been discussed up to this point. You need to know about two school districts that have used narrative theory models for at least three years. I have personally witnessed their success stories, as school leaders and central office leaders strove to supplement their talent searches with more creativity, rigor, and thoughtfulness about searching for the attitudes and dispositions behind their applicants. Let's acquaint ourselves with the Elm Grove Central School District experience, which is outlined in Chapter 7.

Reference

Danielson, C. (2007). *Enhancing professional practice: A framework for teaching,* 2nd Edition. New York: Association for Supervision and Curriculum Development.

# Hiring the Best in the Elm Grove Central School District

We have started to really look carefully at the role of using narratives, not only within our hiring practices, but for staff development, in-service training, and even for the evaluation of our own progress, as a board of education. I have worked with our Board of Education for almost five years now, but it has only been in the last three years that we have started to see some of the fruits of our labor regarding using narratives for bettering our work. It is a process that takes time. Nothing can happen overnight. Staff members have actually commented to me that reading professional stories is fun. Like no other way to learn, they say that they can relate, re-think, and come up with new ways of thinking about their reading instruction, assessment models, and course of action to help kids even more when they look at the professional commentaries of what other teachers do through their written stories of reflection. I love brainstorming with my interview committees on what we should create for our applicants because it does something more for our great school district. It unifies us to get on the same page of what we personally believe about a topic and what we professionally believe about a topic. Sometimes, those two different roles can elicit deeper discussions among my faculty. They think things through as an educator and as a parent. The whole narrative process is actually pretty exciting and a type of tool that I wish I used years ago.

(Dr. Edward Jones, Elm Grove Central School District Superintendent)

The Demographics and History of Elm Grove

Dr. Jones is the third superintendent that Elm Grove has had in 12 years. The district turnover rate for teachers and leaders has gone through many stages of ups and downs due to the district's failure to implement action plans for improving student instruction. Prior to his arrival, there seemed to be a lack of intentional leadership.

While Dr. Jones has been with the district for the last five years much has been accomplished, due to his commitment to looking at new ways of learning, thinking, and decision-making.

Elm Grove is a smaller, very wealthy district in New York State. Approximately 3,000 students attend school across five elementary schools, one middle school, and one high school within the district. The school has been successful over the years even though there was a great turnover of staff in previous years under a different superintendent. Increased student achievement is attributed to the leadership of Dr. Jones and the commitment of the faculty. State Assessment scores have been proficient; yet in 2011, scores plateaued. The graduation rate at the high school exceeds 95% each year.

Technology is of high importance to the Elm Grove administration, and students have had many opportunities to advance their global technology awareness. A local business, Broad Scape Technologies, contributes money to the school district, having established a partnership with Elm Grove in 2009 under the previous superintendent's leadership. The partnership executes a mentor program for all levels of school age children in Elm Grove. Broad Scape is responsible for setting up computer services and software technologies for major industries around the world and it decided to have a local impact by supporting the Elm Grove community.

Last year, Broad Scape supplied each student in Elm Grove with a wireless Chromebook, along with paid training on how to help teachers carry out their instruction to better utilize technological integration. The mentor program has assisted many female students in Grades 10–12 to recognize the importance of pursuing a STEM career (involving science, technology, engineering and mathematics) and to advance such an interest in their ultimate career decisions after graduating from Elm Grove. Last year, 33 female graduates (out of a class of 290 students) expressed an interest in pursuing a career in math and science and they were accepted into four-year colleges to begin their studies within STEM areas of study.

Elm Grove is a moderately diverse school district. While 65% of students are white, 25% of students are black, and about 10% are Pacific-Islander. Very few students receive free or reduced lunches. Females outperform males on most high-stakes tests, as well.

Hiring in the Elm Grove Central School District

The staff at Elm Grove has seen a large turnover rate due to various retirements over the last three years and the dismissal of probationary teachers who had "low scores" on their students' assessment results. Just last year, 22 teachers resigned at the secondary level and eight teachers resigned at the elementary level. Fifty percent of the turnover had to do with retirements. Elm Grove has been quite busy in their hiring responsibilities. Appropriately, Broad Scape mentors have sat on the interview teams of Elm Grove for the past three years.

In 2007–2008, Elm Grove experienced a different, peculiar turn of events within their teaching staff ranks. Approximately 10 staff members were either dismissed or resigned from their teaching positions due to their poor performance or inability to keep up with the increasing job demands of leading their classrooms. Dr. Jones strongly believes that the number one factor for increasing student achievement is attributed to hiring the best staff members possible and then developing their skills throughout their career.

As a result, Dr. Jones re-invented all hiring procedures in Elm Grove and has taken an active role since 2010 in working with all interview teams at each school so that a thorough process for hiring any new staff members is carried out.

The "Old" Hiring Process

Prior to Dr. Jones entering Elm Grove, the process of recruiting and hiring new staff members was archaic. Elm Grove had one lawsuit in 2001 regarding an alleged violation of not being an "equal opportunity employer" (EOE) and allegedly attacking the candidate with slanderous allegations that would ruin his chances of ever finding a teaching job. It led to a major lawsuit that took place for over two years.

The situation had to do with a black candidate who claimed that the Elm Grove interview committee violated his rights during an interview at Johnson Middle School. Inappropriate questions were asked by many committee members as a follow up to a formal interview question about handling a student bullying scenario/example.

Notes were taken by committee members during the interview session that suggested that this candidate would use corporal punishment to problem-solve a student bullying incident if it were to happen in his classroom. This falsification of the candidate's answer was then shared by one committee member outside the interview team's forum, through informal social gatherings outside of school, and as a result, word spread throughout the community that this candidate would use force to stop students from bullying one another. The reputation of this candidate was certainly on the line.

Obviously, such an event ruined the candidate's chances of ever being hired as a teacher, and since this allegation affected a black candidate, the candidate's lawyer also alleged that this was a racist act to purposely bar the black candidate from ever being hired in the district. Ultimately, the black candidate won his lawsuit against Elm Grove due to the recovered notes that were ordered to be released, but the candidate ended up moving out of state due to the long court battle and negative community press, which made living in Elm Grove unbearable.

The *old process* of hiring personnel, even before the 2001 lawsuit, included a mysterious five steps.

The assistant superintendent for personnel (a former mayor of Elm Grove) would do the following.

1. Talk with building principals about any vacancies that might be open throughout the year.
2. Check to see if anyone would be entitled to come back to Elm Grove to fill such a vacancy if they were on a Preferred Eligibility List (PEL). If no one could come back, the job was posted in the classified section of the *Elm Grove Daily News*, the community's smallest newspaper, for only one day.
3. After the deadline to apply closed, the assistant superintendent for personnel would go through all applications and send the top six applicants to the building principals. No one ever knew why "six" candidates were always chosen for interviews, nor did anyone know why they were being moved forward.
4. Building principals would then interview all six candidates by using a committee of no more than three other staff members selected by the principal to represent the school. They then had to send the top four candidates to the superintendent for a final interview. The committee had to send four candidates at all times. This was strictly enforced.

The committee was not allowed to rank the four candidates sent to the superintendent for review. Reference checks were never conducted by anyone other than the assistant superintendent for personnel. If there were "poor" references at this stage of the process, the candidates would be disqualified and whoever was still left out of the four finalists would be interviewed by the superintendent, who would then make a recommendation to the Board of Education.

5. The superintendent would send the final candidate through the board of education approval process at their monthly meetings. The building principal would be made aware of the decision immediately after the meeting took place, for formal approval. Many principals would attend the board of education meetings to find out whom they were going to have as a new staff member so they didn't have to wait until the next day to find out. This enraged the school leaders mostly because there was no trust or communication among the superintendent and the principals.

This process was not only secretive and mysterious, but it certainly did not use any innovative techniques to mine for hiring the best possible teacher or school staff member. Elm Grove has had a long history of nepotism and favoritism in hiring their key teaching positions or support staff positions. Family members and relationships that overlapped with one another across other influential families in the community dominated the landscape of who was ultimately hired in Elm Grove.

Elm Grove's reputation for hiring personnel was a public joke and everyone knew it. When student teaching placements came up through the ranks of the local colleges, no one was interested in student teaching in the district—especially if they didn't have any local ties to any of the influential families in Elm Grove. The number of applications for posted positions decreased by 65% in 1999 and by 72% in 2001—at the time of the Elm Grove lawsuit. Today, Elm Grove has approximately 50% more applicants for every posted teaching position and Dr. Jones' process for screening and recruiting potential candidates is highly respected in his community. It is also worth mentioning that the previous long-standing assistant superintendent for personnel retired in 2003.

Let us now look at Dr. Jones' new approach for hiring personnel and how using narrative theory supplements his talent searches.

New Hiring Opportunities and Narrative Interests

Dr. Jones not only believes that Elm Grove deserves the best teachers and school staff, but he believes that Elm Grove deserves a fair and thorough process for hiring staff members. He believes that his interview teams should be able to "know each and every candidate that they interview, intimately, before the process ends even if they are a complete stranger to Elm Grove" (June 2013 interview). Dr. Jones is also not a stranger to hiring candidates based on their demonstrated knowledge, skills, abilities, and attitudes. He understands narrative theory and although he does not outline an exact process for using narratives to search for desired workplace attitudes, he uses many of the strategies outlined in this book to make clear and intentional decisions about whom he ultimately hires.

Dr. Jones has an incredible relationship with his seven-member Board of Education and they highly respect his expertise. Dr. Jones' doctoral work included interviewing special education teachers and reporting their perceptions related to increasing student achievement on state assessments for students with disabilities. He is no stranger to qualitative research.

At Elm Grove, the new process for screening and recruiting applicant/candidates, which was adopted by the board of education in 2008, includes the following five steps.

1. All of the key administrators from every school in the district and the central office meet monthly to discuss potential vacancies that might occur at any time. Elm Grove takes the hiring of any long-term substitute just as seriously as the hiring of any anticipated probationary appointments, which are usually conducted each March for the upcoming school year.
2. Through these collaborative discussions, Dr. Jones believes that everyone should be involved with identifying the need for staffing due to the vision that Elm Grove has in hiring for total organizational quality. In other words, what is a good hire for one school should be a good hire for another school within their district. Therefore, any employee should be flexible and sensitive to the unique culture of each school. With a very open process for enabling teachers to transfer among

buildings at Elm Grove each year, it is important that the leadership team be involved with the interview process of all staff even if it doesn't directly affect their school at that point in time.

3. As the leadership team identifies a needed position, Dr. Jones places multiple recruitment documents and postings both within the school district and outside the school district. These include posting positions in all local newspapers, colleges, universities, and even supermarkets. Although Elm Grove has a computerized system for posting positions and enabling candidates to apply to Elm Grove on-line, Dr. Jones still believes in advertising positions using paper methods in rare places that his community will spot as they go about their daily life.

4. Once the position is posted and applicants have applied, a team of Elm Grove staff members is assembled to begin discussing criteria for the position. Key areas are identified as themes for creating interview questions further in the process. These key area themes are only categorical and include a topic for the committee to then create questions once the process is furthered along. While Elm Grove does not invite all applicants to a pre-screening process in a central location prior to any interview being conducted, Dr. Jones strives to establish a screening process that is fair and objective through e-mail and website modalities.

5. Key area themes are then turned into interview questions. For example, if a key area theme is "differentiated instruction," then that theme is either turned into an interview question or a story-narrative that will become one of three to five narrative questions. These narrative questions are given to the interviewee after the formal interview takes place at the committee level.

If Elm Grove has 50 applicants for a posted position, of those 50 applicants, Dr. Jones usually reports that about 10 applicants are either not certified or do not have a complete application. An "incomplete" application means that at least one or more of the required documents to apply for the position were not submitted. The required submissions and required attachments for applying on-line at Elm Grove include:

- a complete on-line application
- a cover letter

- a résumé
- copies of all transcripts (unofficial are fine)
- at least three reference letters
- phone contacts for at least four additional professional references and four personal references
- answers to three essay questions pertaining to three constructed narrative essays authored by Elm Grove.

Elm Grove uses a scale or rubric to assess all items within this list (including the last item)—and this is primarily conducted by Dr. Jones and one other interview committee member (for checks and balances). If the pool of 40 applicants is narrowed down to 20 applicants who have also fared well on the checklists and narratives, they are invited to a "meet and greet" screening interview with Dr. Jones and the respective union official who leads the bargaining unit where the new staff member will be placed.

As you can see, the Elm Grove Central School District takes hiring incredibly seriously. Narrative approaches help to narrow down their applicant pools and, as a result, Elm Grove gets a sense of the intimate attitudes of their candidates—some of which are already identified before they meet them in the formal interview stage.

Let us look more closely at the narratives used by Elm Grove at two stages of their hiring processes (both the on-line narrative essay component questions and the formal interview narratives used) regarding their search for a high school business teacher and middle school assistant principal.

Hiring the Best Business Teacher

Webster Street High School has over 1,000 students in Grades 9–12. The school has an incredible sports team and a state-of-the-art technology program, including a graphics design lab and an art lab. It also has one distance learning lab. Students carry netbooks as the building has wireless internet, due to a capital improvement project that passed in 2010 under Dr. Jones' leadership.

Student attendance is impeccable and teachers enjoy teaching at Webster Street. Since 1980, Mrs. Farrow had worked as a business teacher at the school. Due to her parents living out of state in Florida and since the demands of traveling had become increasingly difficult for her over the past few years, Mrs. Farrow felt that it was time to finally retire so she could move to Florida to help her parents during their elderly years.

Mrs. Farrow had a great career at Webster Street. Students loved her, parents loved her, and she brought innovations to the program, including distance learning opportunities through some of her grant writing successes, which benefited the school. Assembling an interview team was a bit emotional for some of the teachers in the school, who were saddened by Mrs. Farrow's retirement announcement, but it didn't stop the school from taking on the task of hiring a new business teacher—a very serious task for Dr. Jones and his staff.

Mrs. Farrow used to teach sections of business in the International Baccalaureate Program that the school set up in 2012. Much of the course design included internships with local businesses, international distance learning projects with a teacher in Japan (who was a friend of Mrs. Farrow's), and she also ran a course about money management and economic planning in the 21st century.

As part of the application criteria, all applicants had to respond to three narrative samples which supported the mission of the school system in realizing the importance of opening up STEM opportunities for all students. Not expecting that their new teacher would be exactly like Mrs. Farrow, the committee established criteria that would provide a framework for hiring the best teacher possible.

On the interview committee sat: the principal, the assistant principal, a business teacher in the department, a 12th -Grade English teacher, a Broad Scape Technologies mentor, a main office secretary, and three parents of future seniors at the school whose students were going to take business classes in the following school year.

Webster Street believed that their next business teacher must support the following four goals in order to be hired:

1. Use modern technological integration methods for all students.
2. Carry out a national and international focus for preparing students for 21st century skills.
3. Focus learning on hands-on and practical internships.

4. Create learning objectives around real-life problems and situations that call for implementing a realistic business model/plan in order to assist both local and global community markets.

In addition to these four categories, the Webster Street committee also wanted to hire an interesting, expert, and compassionate teacher who had a previous background of working in the private business sector.

The committee set up rubrics for assessing both their screening level applicants and their formal, final interview candidates whose narratives would be aligned with the qualities they desired in their next business teacher. One sample rubric is outlined in Table 7.1, and this was aligned with two of the narratives that were used within the Webster Street process to mine for attitudes.

The narratives used to mine for these four major categories are outlined in Table 7.2 and they represent real examples and philosophies about business and learning.

As you can see, both the rubric and the narratives were aligned with one another.

Here, there are favorable and unfavorable attitudes being illustrated. The business teacher candidates will choose what to answer, and they will be required to demonstrate what they know about modern business and learning philosophies. It will help the committee to understand the attitudes of their candidates regarding business philosophies, classroom learning, and the role that technology plays in educating children. Giving money to a church is nice, but it ignores real solutions to real problems. Local decision-making is nice, but there is a world of markets out there for us to know more about and fully understand. The U.S. dollar is impacted by global events and decisions. Webster Street students need hands-on experiences, not text-book-based learning. What was once learned by Jane is no longer the way of the world. Attitudes can be measured, explained, and realized through these narratives.

To hire a business teacher is to hire a CEO of a corporation, and the students who fill the seats of Webster Street need something beyond the chair of a teacher who sits behind a textbook. Students need ultimate preparation for learning about international markets and significant community or world solutions to real problems. If a candidate does not provide insights and attitudes into those topics, then they might not move forward as the best candidate.

Table 7.1

Theme	Excellent Response 2 points	Adequate Response 1 point	Poor Response 0 points
1. Supports the use of technology integration.	Technology is a vehicle that transports curricular initiatives. Modern technology is used daily to engage students and offer a variety of 21st century learning experiences that can be applied to business contexts.	Technology is important and creative. Technology is activity focused without real application to modern business standards.	Technology use is random and it does not drive modern advances in the curriculum. Technology is novel instead of rigorous for carrying out certain curricular advances.
2. Emphasizes the national and international importance of the business curriculum.	Awareness of global economies drives curricular objectives. A balance of localized and national pursuits creates a sense of the world through technology implementation and forging business relationships overseas.	International economies are important but are not developed in the curriculum. An out-of-context business curriculum does not suit modern needs for carrying out economic relationships around the world.	Awareness of international business goals are lacking. Curricular objectives do not address understanding or interacting with global markets.

3. Believes that practical learning goes hand in hand with classroom instruction.	Important business examples, scenarios, and experiences are carried out with experience-based learning (through practical and realistic internship opportunities or visitations to real-life businesses). A solid plan is conceived for creating such practical knowledge.	Recognition is given to hands-on learning opportunities, but plans or ideas are not developed to carry out direct field-work in the area of business and management.	Classroom instruction dictates students' learning. Hands-on opportunities are either ignored or not justified for increasing student engagement outside of classroom situations.
4. Realizes that learning should solve real, modern problems and end up helping the community in some way.	Curricular initiatives have a purpose beyond the classroom. Real problems are explored and community activism is a necessity, not an additive to student learning.	Modern problems and community awareness is recognized, but ideas are not developed for helping student instruction and participation.	Curricular initiatives ignore social justice and community assistance. Business problems and solutions do not direct students with real, modern practicality. Simple monetary donations to struggling communities do not solve real long-term problems.

Hiring in the Elm Grove Central School District

Table 7.2

Narrative 1:

Business should realize what is important locally, first. The United States of America and Wall Street have their hands in too many cookie jars, and monies are given to many other countries when we really need to rebuild our economy here at home—starting with small businesses. Webster students should realize this as they move forward with learning about business models and possibly becoming established with their own money management and maybe even starting their own business after college. That is what they should learn in their business books in the classroom. Computers are OK, yes, but nothing beats learning from books. That is how I learned and look at me, I own my own highly successful business two miles from Webster—where I attended years ago! I even give back some of my profits to the Webster Lutheran Church that we attend. That is a responsibility of a well-off business woman, as well . . . giving back some money to someone else who needs it.

(Jane, Webster High School Parent and 1986 Alumni)

Narrative 2:

Each year, the world seems to get crazier. I mean, everyone is coming out with a new gadget, a new cell phone, a new whatever. Our kids need the basics, rather than being blind-sided on the newest tech stuff out there. At our business, we stick to the basics. We make software products and people buy them. We help set up business systems and they hire us. We are a U.S. company, do our business in the U.S., and see no real need to spend lots of money to do business overseas. We aren't that big. Companies often bite off more than they can chew. We stick to localized solutions for companies who are trying to use technology. But, how can we get our students involved? Learning the basics is great . . . but what do they do in college? Are we preparing them for the real world? What problems will they tackle and how have we prepared them?

(Broad Technologies Chief Executive Officer)

After implementing these narratives, the Webster Street hiring committee overhauled some of their interview questions to better elicit emotions, attitudes, and dispositions beyond their traditional interview questions, according to Table 7.3.

Small semantic changes or a different approach to asking interview questions not only supplements your narrative creation, but they can also provide insights into what your committee may want to establish as narrative criteria for future levels of the talent search.

Table 7.3

Traditional Interview Questions	Attitude-Based Interview Questions
1. Where did you work prior to becoming a teacher, and what did you learn from that job?	1. What would you say to a student who was interested in a STEM career?
2. Tell us about your philosophy of teaching.	2. How did your private sector experiences influence your public sector goals?
3. Were you ever in a leadership position and if so, what did you learn?	3. What should good leaders do?
4. When did you start working with students, and what do you love about working with high school students?	4. If you were a Webster Street student, what would you expect from your business teacher?
5. What are three things that you can bring to Webster Street High School?	5. Talk about your connections with the private sector and what would best renovate a typical Business curriculum through your connections?

Earlier in this book, I discussed the importance of no one being exempt from the narrative process for finding the best hires. Different levels of school staff should be exposed to different types of narratives. In the case of the Elm Grove Central School District, let's look carefully at the talent search process for recruiting and hiring an assistant principal at Warren Middle School.

Hiring the Best Assistant Principal

Warren Middle School houses over 820 students in Grades 5–8 and is also divided into two houses consisting of grade level teams responsible for delivering instruction in core academic subjects. This school is considered to be a larger sized middle school, and discipline has always been a problem at Warren. This is due to the high turnover in assistant principals assigned to each of the houses over the last 10 years, though the new house assistant principals have been there for approximately four years.

Some assistant principals have been poor quality leaders; others have moved on to principalships in other counties or regions. Therefore, discipline has not been consistent at Warren, and the philosophy of discipline at the school is that the assistant principals should handle all discipline.

Warren has seen some slight progress in their student achievement over the past five years. Results on standardized tests in English have increased 4% over the past two years and standardized tests in math have increased 6% over the past two years. Females outperform males by approximately 37% for each test taken. Minority students struggle with assessments, so there is an achievement gap that Warren must address. Most of the discipline issues come from white or black male students at Warren. Yet, incidents are usually not severe enough to warrant involuntary school transfers or placing students on home instruction until further notice.

Last year, 105 student discipline referrals were written for issues ranging from poor attendance or failure to serve "attendance detention," to not turning in homework assignments, to cyber-bullying, to disrespecting adult authority. As in most schools, bus and cafeteria referrals also made the list, especially since an across-grade-level schedule was created in order to accommodate enough students at a time. Some minor fights have been reported and very few incidents involved racial or bias issues at Warren.

The last assistant principal, Mr. Fields, attempted to set up a positive reinforcement behavior management system across one of the houses first, before seeing if it could be implemented within the entire school. Most of the teachers supported this initiative, but it was mostly conceived and implemented by Mr. Fields himself. Therefore, the process for buy-in was difficult, and rolling out the plan was tedious and rocky for Mr. Fields.

Mr. Fields accepted a position as director of curriculum and instruction in a neighboring school district, and, as a result, his resignation from Elm Grove drove the need for hiring a new assistant principal.

Warren followed the new hiring processes created by Dr. Jones for setting up an interview team, establishing criteria, and setting forth a process where all applicants would be screened through web-based narrative tools if their application materials were submitted before the deadline. The process for initiating a search for the replacement of Mr. Fields was one of the most highly successful talent searches for the Elm Grove Central School District.

The interview team consisted of the house principals, two social workers, an attendance secretary, five classroom teachers, and three parents. Brainstorming criteria for their next hire consisted of the following five desired attributes and attitudes:

1. Knowing the differences between adult driven controversies versus student driven controversies.
2. Being able to deal with past practices by creating new alternatives for managing student discipline.
3. Identifying root causes of perceived problems. Overall, student learning is more important than teaching "responsibility."
4. Leading programs by example and creating a positive atmosphere that is not punitive—this was especially important for the committee.
5. Having feelings, emotions, and attitudes about a deep desire to help a child in distress by searching for root causes in order to find problem-solving strategies.

The Warren interview committee realized that their school needed change and that their staff was "sick and tired" of dealing with the same problems in the same way, and this enabled them to mine for these attitudes about the position. The honesty put forth by the interview committee (which represented these exact staff sentiments) was a step forward in not only changing current practices, but for hiring someone aligned with a new vision for Warren Middle School.

Over 62 applicants formally applied to the Elm Grove Central School District on-line application system regarding their expressed interest in the Warren Middle School assistant principal position. Of those 62 applicants, 60 met all of the required application standards.

These 60 applicants were invited to attend a one-and-a-half hour "meet and greet" screening interview in the Warren Middle School cafeteria. Twelve district level administrators met with candidates and administered a survey instrument regarding best practices for teaching at Warren Middle School, along with two sample narratives—which are outlined in Table 7.4. Out of those 60 applicants, 47 candidates showed up. In order

Table 7.4

Narrative #1:

There is this one student, named Josh, who comes to my class each and every day without anything . . . I mean he doesn't ever have a pencil, paper, or math book with him. It is like he is a ghost drifting through his school day. How does he expect to pass math class if he can't even help himself? He'll have to learn someday that he needs to be responsible for his own learning. I can't 'baby-sit' sixth graders. It is my responsibility as a teacher in Josh's life to teach him the consequences of not being responsible. If he comes to class with nothing, he must come after school to do what he missed in class. If he doesn't come after school, the assistant principal will be involved. Josh has to learn that this is serious business. School is a place for work and he has to come prepared just like he would if he was working in the real world.

(Mr. Trevor, Grade 6 Math Teacher)

Narrative #2:

Alexis is one of my most chronic attendance problems. When she does come to school, she comes late. Other than that, she never walks here with her older brother, Jonathan, who is an 8th grader. Fifth graders should be able to get themselves up in the morning and come to school whether the parents are working or sleeping—especially when she can leave the house with her brother. It is truly affecting her studies, as well. So, I tried calling her parents (to no avail) and then decided to work with Child Protective Services on becoming involved and opening up a case. Alexis was absent from school for 40 days since January! Wow! That is eight weeks of school. I have seen no other student like this at my time here at Warren Middle School and I've been a social worker here for 12 years! Thank God CPS took the case. But, every time they close the case after Alexis' attendance improves, she goes back to her old ways. We might have to now pursue a petition for PINS (Person in Need of Assistance) through the court system. More paperwork and little learning for Alexis. She might have to be retained this year.

(Mrs. Baker, Social Worker)

---

to streamline this process and save time, an e-mail blast could have asked candidates to tackle narrative tasks without having to reserve time for face-to-face meet and greet sessions.

However, the Elm Grove Central School District decided to invite their candidates to a central location instead of using e-mail and website references because the district was also looking for an administrator to substitute at buildings while principals or assistant principals were out sick, on vacation, etc. For the Elm Grove Central School District, this process of meeting candidates face to face accomplished multiple hiring needs.

Candidates met with one administrator from Elm Grove for ten minutes and then were given one hour to complete a 50-question survey and write responses to the two narratives which are outlined below. Standard directions, similar to those directions posted on the sample narratives displayed in Chapter 6, reiterated the process required by Elm Grove for applicants completing these narrative tasks.

These narratives aim to uncover candidates' potential attitudes about the established criteria at Warren Middle School. Again, there are favorable answers and there are unfavorable answers depending on how candidates responded to both of these narratives.

In what ways will candidates perceive Josh's low homework turn-in rate? How will candidates view detention and the role of the assistant principal? Does Mr. Trevor pose real issues with real targeted points? Are his viewpoints "wrong-headed" in the eyes of the interview committee members? If a student doesn't have a pencil, can't the teacher simply provide one, or are there deeper issues behind the context of this narrative?

Should Alexis' poor attendance be viewed differently in the second narrative example? In what ways will the new assistant principal view this scenario and make different recommendations for assisting Alexis' family in order to better support her with coming to school on a regular basis? Were steps taken to visit Alexis' house, put a plan together, pick her up for school by using a district bus, etc., or should she be responsible for getting to school on her own? What are the attitudes from the candidates about these scenarios? Do they feel Mrs. Baker's pain, or do they want to truly help Alexis before taking more drastic steps with filing an application for a local law enforcement program for supportive intervention?

The Warren interview committee believed that there were insightful elements portrayed within these narratives and that the candidates who asked thoughtful questions about this narrative, took a pro-child approach, and didn't support punitive decision-making measures would prevail. Furthermore, the committee felt that they could locate a quality assistant principal who would seek alternative problem-solving techniques to put together a plan of action that would not only help Alexis come to school, but have her feel good about coming to school because she would see that everyone who was directly involved actually cared about her. Students often do not see Child Protective Services or law enforcement interventions as signs of "caring."

Rubric-based assessments were used for the narrative portion of this screening task. A sample of such "desired" and "undesired" responses is outlined in Table 7.5.

Obviously, zero-point responses are weak; these attitudes do not align themselves with what Warren desired in their new assistant principal. Whether or not detention, suspension, CPS, or law enforcement interventions were sometimes used as problem-solving approaches in some situations, the Warren committee looked for something different. They wanted those measures to be complete last-resort strategies. It was their prerogative to have an assistant principal who would bring about change at their school. They established benchmark attitudes that were compassionate, non-punitive, positive, and thoughtful when determining how to best help children. Then, and only then, would a candidate become their best hire.

Finally, the interview committee decided to ask the following questions that would mine for attitudes and dispositions in addition to their typical questions which would mine for knowledge, skills, and abilities. In Table 7.6, notice some of the committee members' thoughts about what to anticipate in candidates' responses.

All of these questions dig deeper for attitudes and dispositions using the four SLAC creeds (on students, learning, achievement and culture). Your best school-staff hire would need to demonstrate a greater understanding and articulation of the desired attitudes that your committee is looking for during the talent search process. It is important to uncover these now, as these could be the kinds of deeply rooted attitudes that may very well not be remediated over time.

The Results

Dr. Jones' revised talent search process provided deeper insights and greater results for the Elm Grove community. Both the new business teacher at Webster Street High School and the new assistant principal at Warren Middle School were highly successful and are both completing their fifth year of teaching and leading. What if Dr. Jones had not implemented narrative theory models or tools as a part of his hiring repertoire? Might he still

Table 7.5

Benchmark Criteria	Excellent Response 2 points	Adequate Response 1 point	Poor Response 0 points
1. Adult actions and decisions strive to be positive and supportive.	Dealing with adult processes and treatment of students is well defined. Punitive outcomes are shunned within the narrative responses.	Navigating between adult and student perspectives create an outlet beyond simple support for punitive measures.	Lack of homework leading to school discipline is supported. Interventions prior to CPS or PINS are not clear or well defined.
2. Deeper root causes of problems are analyzed.	A thorough analysis of what appears to be the issue is uncovered to be more than the presented issue. Homework and attendance become symptoms to other larger problems that are looked into more deeply.	The acknowledgment of other issues pertaining to homework or attendance is included in the narrative response.	Teaching responsibility is supported. An agreement with both narratives sustains current status quo culture.
3. Creative alternatives to solving problems are displayed.	An action plan is well defined and offers new avenues into solving root causes that may affect child.	Evidence of moving from only phone contact with parents is mentioned within narratives.	Forging relationships with parents and students are not goals. Muscling outcomes do not have the long-term effect of helping families to help themselves.

(continued)

Table 7.5 (continued)

Benchmark Criteria	Excellent Response 2 points	Adequate Response 1 point	Poor Response 0 points
4. A sense of helping the child is most important.	Deep compassion for helping child and family is evident.	Some acknowledgment of child's feelings and helping child to overcome barriers is mentioned.	Little to no mention of the child within narrative responses exists.
5. Punitive measures take a back seat to positive outcomes.	Positive measures are outlined as part of the action plan for helping to ensure successful outcomes. Detention, suspension, etc. are ineffective measures that have no long-term impact. A happy ending is forecasted for the child and family.	Some mention of punitive school discipline as either being prematurely handled or not necessary appears in the narratives. Does not demonstrate alternate plans, however.	Hierarchical adult behaviors are sustained or supported (i.e. assistant principal decreed student detention, suspension; teacher decreed detention).

have hired quality staff members? Would the Elm Grove hiring process, as it used to exist, still locate quality staff? Some might question whether the support tool of using narratives, as a multiple measure for carefully looking at talent search results, is important if hiring tools can include more thoughtful questions for the interviewees.

The problem with *not* using narrative tools is that you may not be getting the clear insights into attitudes and dispositions that can be found through the art of storytelling. Sometimes a candidate possesses attitudes that we may not be truly aware of, and which pertain to important organizational belief systems about students, learning, assessment, and culture. Again, stories uncover the individual's innermost emotions and attitudes, which we should be able to explore before finding the best hire.

Table 7.6

Attitude-Based Interview Questions
1. How does one train to become an assistant principal? (Is the answer too vague or academic-based? Does the candidate say, "Boy, it's all about on-the-job experience!")
2. Talk about a time when you had to correct negative adult (staff member) behavior? (Does the answer illustrate frustration? Is there a process involved? Are reasons generated for displaying correct behaviors?)
3. What is your ideal dress code for teachers? (Is the answer realistic and modern?)
4. What kinds of things do you let kids get away with? (Is the answer too risky? Is the answer too rigid?)
5. Who should be a member of the school-wide shared-decision-making team? (Are students mentioned?)
6. Tell us something about your own childhood while attending school. (Does the answer focus on something positive or negative?)

Sometimes, the process can be even more powerful than the final product. Look at what the Elm Grove Central School District learned about themselves by establishing benchmark criteria, convening before positions were posted, and learning more about the changes that they desired to make while identifying their innermost feelings about how children should be treated.

Elm Grove has been successful for the last five years when using narrative tools as part of their talent search. They had filled over 50 positions prior to the summer of 2015. The success rate of their new personnel ranks at 98%, while just 2% of new hires struggled with curriculum construction or curriculum integration for carrying out the Common Core State Standards. The new Elm Grove staff members have been highly successful on all evaluations, participation in professional development opportunities, collaboration among staff, and participation on school reform subcommittees.

In Chapter 8, you will meet the Gardenville City School District where poverty and deep community problems were crying out for the best and brightest staff members who could demonstrate attitudes about reform in order to lead their school district through the turmoil while also striving to increase student achievement.

Hiring the Best in the Gardenville City School District

I expect Gardenville to assist with taking care of our students when they are not home. Most of them don't want to be at home anyway. I see the kids coming to school and hanging out near the school doors sometimes two or two-and-a-half hours before school even starts. Some of the kids hold the doors open for the teachers when they arrive to school because they want so badly to come in. The drugs and violence in our community is crippling and I am always worried about these kids getting hurt. They need caring, inspiring teachers who are role models. They need more caring than you can possibly imagine. They deserve more.
(Donna, Canton Elementary School Parent-Teacher Association President)

The Demographics and History of Gardenville

Gardenville is a very unique city school district. Thirty-five community schools house students from Pre-K through Grade 5 while Gardenville middle and high schools have no magnet school possibilities. The ethnic background of the school district includes an immigrant population (predominantly Hispanic) which often scores very low on standardized tests, unfortunately. The percentage of inner city students who receive free or reduced-price meals is 68% and the Caucasian population of students in the district is 36%.

Gardenville has much industry, however, so donations from these industries help Gardenville—property taxes do not fund the school district program as is normally the case according to state guidelines for city school districts and funding regulations.

Gardenville hiring processes are incredibly archaic. The process is limited, non-collaborative, and principal-based. Each school principal in Gardenville has complete autonomy over whom they hire each year.

Some Gardenville principals have been accused of hiring family members, friends, or acquaintances. One Gardenville principal was investigated for taking monetary bribes in support of hiring only certain people to fill various teaching vacancies.

Interviews are incredibly irrelevant—whereby questions, answers, rating scales, etc. have no sound documentation procedures or methods. Principals try to recruit quality educators, but the success rate of educators finishing their probationary appointments, despite nepotism, is well below a 50% success rate, mainly because central office staff members conduct one out of every three evaluations for all staff members each year and they weed out the low quality teachers who may have been hired by the principals in the first place. Hiring training was conducted by a new superintendent of schools in 2013, but union officials were not in agreement with all of the steps outlined in such training.

This chapter does not focus on uncovering Gardenville's flawed process for hiring, but it rather focuses on a success story of one principal, named Mr. Carey, at Canton Elementary School, who believes that attitudes are incredibly important when making hiring decisions. Mr. Carey still continues to infuse narrative theory into his interview process in order to mine for the attitudes and dispositions of his applicants/candidates. Mr. Carey has used narrative theory models for approximately four years and he has hired over 50 staff members across the district during his tenure in three different schools.

This chapter looks at the outcomes of two specific hires (a reading teacher and a social worker) and argues that in reality it is likely that narrative theory could have supplemented hiring processes in all of the district schools if a disagreement between the district and the union regarding formalizing a hiring process had not taken place. However, narrative theory models are fully endorsed by seven of the district schools and have informally been part of their practices at the same time that Mr. Carey has formalized these same practices over the past four years with a 97% success rate.

The Story of Canton Elementary School

Canton does not want to be defined by its poverty even though some of its staff members are becoming "burnt out" due to the economic realities of working with their students. The teachers care for their students by providing them with clothes, food, and emotional support. Canton teachers take their work home and think about their students' lives each and every day when they leave their school, but this is not necessarily a bad type of "burnout."

The Canton PTA is highly involved but devotes a larger part of its operating budget to feel-good prizes they hope will entice the kids to come to school. Mr. Carey has a different vision, and wants to prioritize education programming and support for the school's academic needs.

Mr. Carey does not believe that it is a school's job to "take care" of students (with toys and knick-knacks) while they are away from home. Instead, Mr. Carey believes that it is a school's job to help kids learn. Sometimes, Mr. Carey and Donna (the PTA President) exchange laughs about their disagreements regarding the primary purpose of a school.

Mr. Carey knows that Donna is a saint at heart and they work together incredibly well even though they have different philosophies about public schooling. Mr. Carey lived in poverty as a child, so he is well attuned to the daily struggles that his students face. Mr. Carey believes that his primary message to his students is: "This is your life now, but prepare yourself with an education to change this life forever."

While Mr. Carey has complete autonomy over his hiring procedures, like all of the other Gardenville principals, his interview questions differ from his colleagues' interview questions.

Table 8.1 lists the questions Mr. Canton used to hire a physical education teacher.

In this case, Mr. Carey's narrative tools actually helped him to come up with some interview questions that would also mine for attitudes about various topics. The questions go deeper than "How can you help an obese student?" or "How do you perceive jocks?" Those questions are too leading and they actually help a candidate to answer the way that an interview team would expect them to be answered. From hiring physical education teachers to teacher aides to reading teachers, the power behind narrative models are extremely useful for finding the very best school staff member for your organization.

Hiring the Best Reading Teacher

Mr. Carey was faced with hiring a new reading teacher and a new social worker in 2013. Let's consider looking at some factors that could influence student achievement according to Mr. Carey's beliefs about learning

Table 8.1

Attitude-Based Interview Questions
1. Tell me about your own experiences in physical education classes and what you now wish to do the same or differently from those past classes that you took when you were a child.
2. Discuss your attitudes about state mandates for physical education requirements.
3. What are your thoughts about grading students in your physical education classes?
4. What are your attitudes about students who play football? Golf? Yoga? Cheerleading?
5. How do you feel about obese students needing to complete the same course requirements as their peers who are not obese?
6. Should students with poor grades be able to continue participating in extracurricular activities or playing a sport?

and instruction (which naturally fell into the four SLAC creeds on students, learning, achievement and culture).

1. Good teachers *provide regular feedback* to students so they know how they are progressing in class.
2. Good teachers *collect comprehensive learning data* on their students and use data to make specific instructional decisions for what their students need to do next.
3. Good teachers believe that special education services can be made possible *only if all other avenues have been explored* prior to making a Committee on Special Education (CSE) referral.
4. Good teachers *do not believe* that simply "completing work" leads to success.

Mr. Carey felt that providing constant feedback to his students was absolutely essential at Canton. Many, if not all, other teachers at Canton provide feedback and assist students to set up portfolio tracking charts so students can track their own progress. Table 8.2

illustrates how these practices were transformed into real stories by the Canton interview team which mined for the candidates' attitudes about topics or policies that the school wanted to consistently implement across the entire school.

Table 8.2

Narrative #1:

We all know that Sarah has reading comprehension difficulties. I mean, that is old news. We have tried everything with her, but she just doesn't get it. At this rate, we might as well refer her to our building child-study team and get her some special education services. I have tried giving her multiple choice tests to see how she does. The reading teacher has also tried. We are still scratching our heads to come up with ideas for reading interventions and the longer we take to compile more data, the longer Sarah will suffer with her reading. Let's just get her referred and go from there. Sarah's parents are already on board with the special education route, so we are OK to get going . . . like right now!

(Mr. Jacobs, Grade 6 Teacher)

Narrative #2:

It is hard to always explain a topic in many different ways so that everyone can understand it. I mean, sometimes not everyone "gets it" and I have to move on. That is life. It doesn't mean that one child is smarter than the next; it just means that if I tried to get all students to get everything at every single moment, we would be stuck on one chapter in the book all year long. If kids struggle, they can always read the textbook on their own—even outside of class.

(Miss Arlington, Grade 4 Teacher)

Narrative #3:

My students and their parents receive a ton of feedback throughout the school year. We have quarterly report cards and five-week progress reports that are mailed home. Throw in a parent conference each year and that amounts to many opportunities that students (and their parents) can receive feedback. No one can say that we didn't warn them that their child is failing. This happens every year in our school. Students who don't do their work should know that there is no way that they can possibly pass, so if they approach their teachers surprised that they did not do well, all the teachers can do is shake their heads and show them all of the times that they tried to help them. You have to "do" in order to "pass." This is common sense even at our poor school.

(Mrs. Quinn, Social Worker)

Again, these narratives elicited responses and expressions about special education services, providing feedback to students, remediation philosophies, and parent communication. Is it ethical to work with a parent behind the scenes and convince them to employ special education services, perhaps prematurely? When there was any deviation from valuing what Canton believed as an organization regarding these core beliefs and values that the interview team defined as their standards for working with students and parents, then the candidate was disqualified as an applicant. Out of a field of 355 applicants for the one open position for a reading teacher, 128 applicants did not move to the next round within Mr. Carey's talent search.

The process of finding candidates who also believe in these topics as "best attitudes" or "best practices" for becoming a collaborative reading teacher at Canton leveraged Mr. Carey to find his ideal choice for hire and the committee agreed with his choice. Remember, attitudes are often difficult to remediate. Mr. Carey did, indeed, innovate some attitude mining for hiring the best possible staff members beyond the scope of examining their résumés and transcripts.

Since adopting narrative theory models in 2012, Gardenville has interviewed candidates for approximately 135 vacant positions among the 11 total schools (including Canton). It has had a job success rate of 97%—measured by the employees' evaluations, day-to-day on-the-job attitudes, mentor assessments, portfolio requirements, and qualitative awareness of social integration into the schools as a successful, contributing, collaborative team member. These results have led 10 other school districts to adopt narrative theory models as part of their hiring processes. While several of the districts are still working out collective bargaining agreements to define interview and hiring requirements, there is no dissension concerning the use of narratives in the process. The 97% success rate is an impressive one.

Four percent of the total new hires moved on to new positions in other school districts and 1% of those new hires had circumstances out of their control which required them to resign from their positions (i.e. family matters, moving to a different location with their families, life events, such as the death of a spouse, etc.). While narrative tools were not necessarily the only reason for this high success rate, the story-lines embedded within the narratives captured hundreds of attitudes from thousands of applicants about what Gardenville believed a new staff member should have as foundational feelings and beliefs before they even entered their school district.

Hiring the Best Social Worker

Mr. Carey relies heavily on his social worker. His previous social worker, Mrs. Williams, was a hub of the Gardenville community. Mr. Carey learned that Mrs. Williams became ill and as a result, she needed to go on sick leave for an undetermined amount of time. This took place during the middle portion of Mr. Carey's 2012–2013 school year. As he sought to replace Mrs. Williams, he wanted to establish similar characteristics and philosophies that Mrs. Williams' carried out each day. He absolutely loved her working style and wanted to mine for the same attitudes that Mrs. Williams embodied. Obviously, Mr. Carey knew that he wasn't trying to clone Mrs. Williams, but to acquire a new social worker, who had similar attitudes about students, learning, achievement, and cultural implications about school success, was something that Mr. Carey and his team desperately wanted. Some of the attitudes that Canton mined for included the following target statements written by the interview team:

- Looking beyond the walls of the school to make connections with families is extremely important.
- Being compassionate, but firm, will help students focus on learning as their number one priority, rather than wallowing in their own realities of tough home-life situations during times when students should be learning.
- Being a proactive problem-solver. This would enable the social worker to prevent situations from happening because of his understanding of the intricate dynamics of Canton families, rather than having to react to emergencies or situations after the fact.

These were the three most important attitudes that the interview committee and Mr. Carey loved about Mrs. Williams and desired for their next social worker hire. Mr. Carey recruited over 138 applicants and used screening narratives as a tool to locate candidates with the best attitudes for Canton and to disqualify candidates with attitudes that did not fit into Canton's belief system.

As a result, one particular narrative was created about Jacob (a pseudonym). This illustrates a typical day depicting what this student went through and how the school decided to either handle or not handle working with this child. Table 8.3 illustrates the reflection process that this narrative initiated for getting to the heart of what applicants felt about their own governing philosophies regarding schools and learning.

Here, baby-sitting Jacob and exclusively focusing on providing the basic needs for Jacob was only positioning Canton as "caretaker" instead of the school being known as a learning institution. While Canton was certainly empathetic to Jacob's life, the school culture strives to make learning a number one priority.

Compassion and love are important. Mr. Carey believes that. But, Mr. Carey is also trying to set up a school that would make students proud, not a school where staff would be allowed to enable students into feeling as if their lives were dealt to them unfairly. Instead, Canton strives to empower students, to make their lives better than they were, to grow and learn in important ways so that their futures will be based on incredible schooling—a way for students to enter into the world with confidence.

Table 8.3

> *Poor Jacob . . . I love this little guy so much. He cannot possibly even think about math when he doesn't even have a bed to sleep in at night or food to eat. When he comes down to my office because he has been misbehaving in class, I just hug him and try to help him take away all of his daily pains and thoughts about going home. He seems to come into school more depressed each day. I've tried calling his mother, but she never gets back to me.*
>
> *I don't expect Jacob to get much of anything done because school work is just the tip of his iceberg. He cannot possibly think about doing school work or homework when he hardly has a home to go home to. He certainly cannot eat dinner at home, either, because there is hardly any food. CPS was involved a while back, but Jacob's mom is a good excuse-maker and deceiver. Magically, she had boxes of cereal on her counter one day when CPS came by. At least when Jacob comes to school, we can talk for hours, feed him, have him wash up, and play some games together. He needs a big sister figure. I'm glad to help this little guy.*
>
> *(Mrs. Wilcox, Grade 2 Teacher)*

Notice the language in each of the rubric categories found in Table 8.4 as Canton designed what would be "favorable" versus "unfavorable" for their candidates' narrative responses.

Mr. Carey's successful candidate, Miss Chamberlain, embodied core attitudes and dispositions that matched Canton Elementary School. To date, Miss Chamberlain has been a Canton staff member for three years and has mobilized the community to carry out various initiatives on the weekends so that learning could take place in school. From setting up garage sales to sponsoring free meals at the school on Saturdays, Miss Chamberlain discerned the difference between what students need to accomplish in the classroom and what the school can do for students beyond the walls of Canton. Sure, Miss Chamberlain hugs Jacob and gets him breakfast each morning, but the focus when Jacob is in school is to be focused *on school*. Very rarely are board games played because they are now used as rewards, not as the main curriculum.

Narrative Power

In a world where class divisions and the realities of poverty dominate, Mr. Carey is moving Canton forward. As he desires to hire the best possible staff members for his school, he is faced with the need to figure out new ways in which he can gain entry into the hearts of his employment applicants. While systematic methods for traditional hiring are sometimes helpful, Mr. Carey found something more. As attitudes have often been neglected or even ignored during older talent searches, Mr. Carey believes that narrative models are incredible ways to supplement his tool kit for hiring personnel:

> *I wouldn't have believed it at first. Talent searches are time-consuming, in themselves. I've always thought that I asked great interview questions, but after thinking about using narratives just to get a bit more out of knowing my applicants, I look back and remember some people that I hired and some of the challenges that I faced. Some of them aren't here anymore; some transferred out. I'm not saying that narratives would have solved any problems that came about; I'm just saying that in our professional*

Table 8.4

Benchmark Criteria	Qualifies	Somewhat Qualifies	Disqualified
1. SW looks beyond school walls to make connections to families.	SW becomes part of the home and works with parents or guardians to problem solve together for making school and home successful places for a child.	SW shows some signs of moving beyond school-based contacts.	SW defaults to either cold or out-of-touch contact attempts (i.e. telephone, etc.).
2. SW is firm and caring.	SW moves beyond emotions of each student case and rather prepares students for learning each day. SW believes that getting students back to class is the most important goal.	Learning is articulated and an attempt to move beyond emotional support is somewhat evident in the narrative response.	Too much emphasis is placed on the state of a students' socio-economic realities. SW is too sympathetic to student realities.
3. SW believes that school is a place for learning and moves this vision forward.	Students are equipped to deal with their realities as the focus on learning is a vision that must be carried out. SW carries out this message along with other staff members and the result is that students articulate this importance.	SW is able to articulate the importance of school and learning, but it doesn't become relevant for the student to become the chief owner of this philosophy.	Taking care of students' basic needs are the only focus of the SW.
4. SW is proactive with problem solving.	SW seeks out parent communication as a monitoring device, rather	SW moves beyond contact, only, and attempts to put	SW only puts out daily fires and focuses on situations

	than using such communications to inform parents about student misbehaviors. SW knows that students will most likely have a bad day before the student comes into the school. The action plan is collaborated with student, family, and school, rather than devised by SW and shared.	a plan of action together for the family.	at that time only, rather than gaining information prior to incidents taking place.

world, we don't really take the time to know more about who we are hiring. We can get a glimpse into their feelings about something . . . their attitudes about a situation. Real situations. Things we struggle with on a daily basis. And . . . our committees have grown together. Our school has grown together. We become more united by constructing the stories that we author each day whether we use our experiences in a talent search or have them as a reference for ourselves . . . a record-keeping trail of how we live in our professional worlds. Stories are really important to us. Really important.

(Mr. Carey, Principal)

Both of Mr. Carey's worlds (professional and personal) overlap as his own identity shifts from using only the traditional methods of pulling out human experiences to using more intricately designed systems for conducting his search for the best attitudes within his candidates.

His goal, then, like that of the Elm Grove Central School District, is to hire the best possible staff member and acknowledge that human perspectives through attitude and disposition storytelling will create an organization that is fully comprehensive in both vision and approach.

PPCs and FAQs

Some of my colleagues, who use narratives for mining attitudes and dispositions during their recruitment and hiring processes, asked me to put together a section about the pluses, potentials, and concerns of using a deep, narrative process as one of many measures used to consider who the "best" employee is for your organization. Therefore, this chapter is devoted to supporting your future work, offering suggestions, and discussing the power that lies ahead for you and your team.

Pluses

First, let's look carefully at the pluses of using narrative theory within talent searches for schools. I gathered qualitative feedback from the hiring committees discussed in this book, as I wanted to learn more about what they thought about their narrative experiences. Here are 30 anonymous comments that were received in the exit surveys in response to one simple question: "What did you like about using narratives in your talent search?"

1. It was fun.
2. I learned more about myself while learning more about the candidates who interviewed with us.
3. I've never done this before and it was well worth my time.
4. What started out as a difficult process is now second nature for our school.
5. Stories are so great for getting to the heart of a matter that we wanted to find out more about what went through our interviewees' minds.

6. I was amazed at some of the responses that our candidates gave to such complex situations. Some answers were awful and some were terrific. It was neat to draw out those differences.
7. I liked doing something different beyond the traditional interviews that we always handled the same way.
8. Never would I have imagined what some of the people said during their interviews.
9. I can't believe that using stories helped me to disqualify some applicants right from the start of my recruitment process when hiring a food and consumer science teacher.
10. When I generally talk to my wife about my experiences using stories on the interview teams at my school, my wife always tells me that she wished she used narratives before we were married!
11. If you follow the process, you can achieve a new lens into your applicants' attitudes.
12. Our team was confused about using narratives at first, but after we took a risk and tried it, we will never go back to our same, usual routines of the past.
13. I'm glad I was involved in such a thoughtful process.
14. I now know more about the English teacher that we finally hired. We actually started talking about co-planning when we saw each other for this first time after the interviews. We hit the ground running on our co-planning which was a narrative that we constructed for our hiring process!
15. So easy. So awesome. I've never done anything like this before, that's for sure!
16. I'm amazed at what we were able to extract from our candidates.
17. Asking questions about science experiments was getting boring. But, when we created a story about the purposes of geology for hiring a science teacher, we turned something boring into an emotional gathering while talking about planet Earth and planet Mars!
18. Who would have thought that reading a story about one of my kiddos would get me all teary-eyed!

19. I think our interview team grew closer together as a result of our hiring process.
20. Amazing, to say the least . . . just amazing!
21. I have become a believer in narrative theory. At first, I thought it was just mumbo-jumbo, some sort of voodoo-magic just for Dr. Jetter to gather some research on what we were doing.
22. My sister who works for First Niagara Bank became interested in narratives after talking to her about what my school did.
23. I can't wait to see how all of this plays out for our upcoming school year. For once, I think we really did hire the best social studies teacher!
24. "No way," I thought. This seemed too time consuming and extraneous. Boy, was I wrong!
25. I really enjoyed how Dr. Jetter came to our school to train us before we did things on our own. Thank you for opening our eyes to storytelling.
26. Some responses to the narratives were helpful; some were not. All in all, however, I do believe that we found something deeper in the person we hired that we would have never known if we didn't use a few stories. Pretty interesting concept.
27. I'd be interested to see some other stories in order to get an idea about different questions or scenarios that could be asked.
28. I think any school could use something like this. We gave it a shot and just went for it. You don't really lose anything by trying it out, and, for us, it worked out very nicely.
29. My team teacher and I are dorks. We now actually use stories to see how we both would respond to a situation. Sometimes it turns into a heated debate, but that gets us closer to the same bottom line of "how will this help kids?"
30. My co-teachers and I are going to use stories for a presentation to our parents on open house night. I'm excited to try this out. I think it'll help our parents to realize the day-to-day stuff we work through while taking care of their children and helping them learn something each day.

From professional development opportunities to open house meetings, I've found that the professionals who work on a narrative project for their interview teams really learn something deeper than they ever thought they would learn. They know their candidates better. In the end, they knew who the "best" was and they hired them.

Potentials

Not only does creating a narrative process within your talent searches have the potential to help you hire the best while moving your team closer together as a unified SLAC crew, but I wonder if we have a duty or a calling to strive to know more about whom we hire. Maybe there is a more sweeping global duty to examine attitudes in addition to the knowledge, skills, and abilities that we mine for when we hire school staff members.

Stories carry the power to examine attitudes. In all of the cases presented within this book and the ones that I am gathering for announcing future narrative successes, we can see a pattern of success taking shape. Stories reflect and refract our emotions and thoughts. They help us to envision our own potential identity shifts and epistemological viewpoints.

The potential of using narrative can perhaps reach across all markets. The comment from one teacher about the expression of interest in narratives from a sister who worked in a bank makes me think about the power of using storytelling in any recruitment and hiring situation. Maybe this kind of research could leave a new legacy in general human resources practices. What I do know is that the more we use narrative and take risks in getting something more from our candidates, the more we will create a vast body of research that will enable us to get deeper insights into the attitudes that drive job searches and recruitment tactics.

Recently, I had a discussion with two chief information officers from two different charter schools. They were intrigued by the potential power that storytelling holds and believed that attitude analysis was very important and something often ignored. So, even a quick discussion with your colleagues could lead to a new revolution of focusing on the importance of personal, professional, and workplace attitudes.

Concerns and FAQs

With the pluses and the potentials of narrative theory entering into talent search processes, it is important to recognize the concerns that might arise from your team members. This section answers some of the most frequently asked questions that I heard from school leaders and interview teams from the schools and school districts discussed in this book. The FAQs will help us to recognize the potential pitfalls of our work, where we need to improve, and where we need to comfortably be if we are going to commit to using narrative theory as a supplementary model within our talent searches.

The comments and questions that follow were expressed through the same exit surveys as used above, with participants responding to the question: "What were some of the complications or concerns while using a narrative process within your talent search?" From the feedback that I received, I created an answers section to address some of those concerns. This will help your team to tackle the tough issues behind using a new process at your school or district. The main concern across all of the interview teams that I have worked with had to do with issues of time and process. Here are six key FAQs and my answers to them:

1. Doesn't the process of using narrative theory within a talent search take too long?
2. Our staff and principal are already swamped. How much additional time does this take—especially during the recruitment phase?
3. How do you go from narrative to rubric? That seems like a difficult task.
4. How in the world can we read everyone's responses and then place those onto a rubric? We will be there all night.
5. How can you get all of the interview team members to agree on what type of narrative to construct?
6. Who is going to take the time to write the narratives? I don't think I can do this on my own because I'm not really a creative writer.

Answers: At first, your team will struggle a bit. You might feel like you are limping to your desk in the morning. It is important to always remember that you are on a search to learn more about the intricate minds and hearts of your candidates. Use that as your motivation. The tasks might seem difficult or challenging, but you will be able to do this. Here is how: first, meeting with your interview team in order to brainstorm your criteria for deciding what characteristics you are looking for in your new best hire only takes one hour, at most. I've seen teams meet for one hour during which they also accomplished deciding what kinds of narratives to author. So set aside one hour. It may feel like you are adding stress to your already hectic schedule, but it is worth every minute in the end. Investing in some time now is better than having to remediate later.

After you create one or two narratives, which takes less than 20 minutes on average, your team can decide who will go through the piles of e-mail responses or papers submitted. This is where you might think things will get very tedious because screening and recruitment processes tend to result in larger numbers of submissions. Don't let this fool you, though. Many applicants do not turn anything in. You can automatically disqualify those applicants. Many submit weak or short responses that do not capture what you are looking for. Those are easy to spot. Here's a quick tip for school leaders and interview teams: create a maximum word limit that is smaller for the screening stage and larger for the interview stage. Many interview committees trust the principal or assistant principal to go through the submissions screening process. For school leaders, this takes some time, but remember, you are already looking at lots of other documents and pieces of the application packets that have already been submitted anyway.

When the interview team moves through using rubrics to diagnose what they are reading, this takes no longer than if the committee passed around a candidate's portfolio and each person took a 10-minute look per candidate. Remember, if you stick to the process and your established criteria, moving from narrative to rubric becomes easier the more you practice. Think about all of those times where you had to correct student exams or assessments. It became easier and easier for you as you rifled through papers because you had a benchmark and knew what you were looking for.

Next, some people think that they are not creative enough to write sample narratives or stories for use during the interview process. Keep the following in mind: if you think of a student or an emotional incident, it will be easy to write those feelings and insights down. After you get those thoughts on paper, worry about playing around with the narrative so it captures everything that was discussed in Chapters 4–5. Your voice will naturally come through as you think about your emotions. Most of the interview teams that I have met found a quasi-story-writing king or queen of the school. If you can find one or two of these types of creative writers, they always love to create something meaningful and useful for their colleagues, especially if it has implications for hiring the best school staff members whom they, too, will have to work with. I've also seen a few school districts offer a contractual stipend for teacher or support staff leaders for carrying out interview facilitation and preparing materials (which also included authoring the narratives to be used by the school). It is extremely easy to come to a "unanimous" consensus on what to mine for because each position is different and staff members respect each other's knowledge of their area. For example, I've seen school psychologists offer some scenarios about areas that only school psychologists would know—the interview teams would automatically let the psychology team get on with creating the sample narratives.

What is unique about this kind of cooperation and professionalism is that it helps staff members to learn more about the craft of teaching, counseling, or repairing something—all of the good stuff that we do for children each and every day. Remember, professional development is an amazing by-product of using narrative models in your hiring batting order.

Words of Advice

The number one thing that I tell school teams is to start slow and to just try one story out as a test run. Some principals use staff meetings as an opportunity to try out narratives on their staff. Slow is OK. Slow is good. If slow is the best that you can do in the beginning of your journey, it is 100% better than not diving in to try the process out at all. Remember, if you try it, things cannot get screwed up. No harm will be done. After all, you are looking for deeper understandings, not "gotcha!" moments to pull one over on your candidates.

The number two thing that I tell interview teams is to map out the steps to the narrative process and set time limits. The Elm Grove Central School District set aside the following time stamps and stayed on track almost perfectly.

- **1 hour:** to brainstorm with interview committee on vacant position and types of narratives to create using the four SLAC creeds.
- **1 hour:** (in addition to the time that you would normally spend on sifting through your candidates during the screening review process) comprising:
  - **20 minutes:** to create the sample narratives. (This might not be part of the committee's duties as stated earlier, should you have a "narrative king or queen" to rely on.)
  - **10 minutes x eight candidates:** to review your interview submissions and place a score on the rubric that was used. (This actually didn't account for additional time when they factored in normal breaks, lunch, interviews that ended earlier, or candidates who didn't even show up! Yes, this happens. You already know this!)

+ _____

= Total additional time to use narrative theory models starting right now: **2+ hours**

I placed a "+" next to the number 2 because when you start out it will take a bit longer until you get the hang of it. But, remember, it is worth every minute. You want the "best" school staff, not the "good," "great," or even "better" staff members. The "best." That's the high bar that will be set.

Finding the "Best" by the End of Your Hiring Process

It is important to remember that *variance can be your enemy*. When you have the best teachers and the worst teachers, something will go wrong. When you have the best principals and the worst principals in a system, something will go wrong. Student achievement will suffer and variance is what holds back organizations from flourishing collectively.

There are poor, fair, good, better, and best employees out there. But, being the best includes having the appropriate knowledge, skills, abilities, and *attitudes*. You are charged with the task of finding the best, not the good, great, or better, but the best school staff members to join your team.

Creating a Viral Process: Looking Outside the School Walls

The process outlined in this book is a learning experience for everyone involved (from principals to staff members to board of education members to superintendents). The brainstorming process of setting up criteria, designing narratives, and also recognizing the evaluation categories that have tiers of "desired responses" and "undesired responses" is essential for mining for attitudes. Stories unpack the power behind human values and positions of the human heart. *Stories become memorable as they become viral.*

Within the stories of the Elm Grove Central School District, the Gardenville City School District, the Huntington School District, the Moorehead Central School District, and Washington Middle School, along with other schools that are using narrative theory models for talent searches, the results have been truly remarkable. With a combined success rate of 97% relative to the hiring and sustainability of many different talent searches conducted across New York State, story-telling or narrative models have increased the knowledge of the interview committees as they mine for their candidates' attitudes about education, policy, and most importantly, children.

The narrative theory model for supplementing an already established talent search process across various states is expected to grow in the upcoming years. As more and more schools utilize this methodology, narratives can be archived and shared with colleagues across the nation. The idea here is that collectively, we all want to hire the very best educators and leaders for our schools. Sharing what works and does not work is just one step in the process of a systems-approach-mindset for educational professionals and researchers.

If there is one final message that I wish to leave you with, it would be "You can do this starting right now." Think of all of the chances that you have had to hire the "best." Think about those situations and re-read Chapter 1. You have control over the *challenges* that exist within talent searches and you have control over the *process* of hiring beyond the knowledge, skills, and abilities that your applicants expect you to search for during your talent searches.

We have not seized the opportunity of providing a deeper soul search while hiring professionals who will be in charge of our children today and tomorrow, but you can change that right now. All it takes is commitment, a little extra time, and a dose of creativity. The results can be astonishing for supplementing the information that assists you to make very important hiring decisions in the future. Most of all, you can discover the hidden feelings and responses behind your new hires' attitudes and dispositions by asking the right questions and authoring the most useful narratives for your school or district. *All it takes is a commitment to search for that which lies within—through the use of a simple story.*

eBooks
from Taylor & Francis
Helping you to choose the right eBooks for your Library

Add to your library's digital collection today with Taylor & Francis eBooks. We have over 50,000 eBooks in the Humanities, Social Sciences, Behavioural Sciences, Built Environment and Law, from leading imprints, including Routledge, Focal Press and Psychology Press.

Choose from a range of subject packages or create your own!

Benefits for you
- Free MARC records
- COUNTER-compliant usage statistics
- Flexible purchase and pricing options
- All titles DRM-free.

Benefits for your user
- Off-site, anytime access via Athens or referring URL
- Print or copy pages or chapters
- Full content search
- Bookmark, highlight and annotate text
- Access to thousands of pages of quality research at the click of a button.

Free Trials Available
We offer free trials to qualifying academic, corporate and government customers.

eCollections
Choose from over 30 subject eCollections, including:

Archaeology	Language Learning
Architecture	Law
Asian Studies	Literature
Business & Management	Media & Communication
Classical Studies	Middle East Studies
Construction	Music
Creative & Media Arts	Philosophy
Criminology & Criminal Justice	Planning
Economics	Politics
Education	Psychology & Mental Health
Energy	Religion
Engineering	Security
English Language & Linguistics	Social Work
Environment & Sustainability	Sociology
Geography	Sport
Health Studies	Theatre & Performance
History	Tourism, Hospitality & Events

For more information, pricing enquiries or to order a free trial, please contact your local sales team:
www.tandfebooks.com/page/sales

www.tandfebooks.com

For Product Safety Concerns and Information please contact our EU representative GPSR@taylorandfrancis.com
Taylor & Francis Verlag GmbH, Kaufingerstraße 24, 80331 München, Germany

www.ingramcontent.com/pod-product-compliance
Lightning Source LLC
Chambersburg PA
CBHW061842300426
44115CB00013B/2476